The Light
in the Middle
of the Tunnel

The Light in the Middle of the Tunnel

Harrowing but Hopeful Stories of Parkinson's Family Caregivers

SUSAN GANGSEI

*And the Many Generous Caregivers
Who Shared Their Stories*

The Light in the Middle of the Tunnel

Copyright 2013 Susan Gangsei

Book design by The Roberts Group Editorial and Design

Front cover art copyrighted by Susan Gangsei

All rights reserved. Published in 2013.

The names and identifying characteristics of the persons whose stories are told in this book have been changed to preserve their privacy.

ISBN 978-0-9890669-0-7

Published by Aston Group, Minneapolis, MN

Requests for information should be e-mailed to Susan@TheLightintheMiddleoftheTunnel.com.

We want to hear from you. Please send your comments about this book to us in care of Susan@TheLightintheMiddleoftheTunnel.com.

DEDICATION

To my husband who took me on a journey of a lifetime.
I love you.

CONTENTS

Introduction   1

I.   **Angry: I Didn't Volunteer for This!**   7

My Story: This Is Not the Deal I Signed Up For   8

The Ventriloquist's Dummy   10

They Don't Have a Clue   12

I Swear Like a Sailor   14

Sati—The Burning of the Widow   16

Two Strikes, But She's Not Out   19

Reflection: Moses Deserved to Go to the Promised Land, Didn't He?   21

II.   **Scared: The Great Unknown**   25

My Story: Control—My Favorite Form of Denial   26

The Great Unknown   28

The Real Question   30

Where's the Hope?   32

The Prophet on the Plane   34

Reflection: Barking at a Snowman   36

III.   **Sad: Where's the Light Switch? It's Dark in Here**   37

My Story: I Knew I Was in Trouble   38

He Seems All Right to Me   39

The World Gets Smaller   41

Which One of Us Is Sick?   43

My Heart Is Forever Broken, But I Can Live with That   45

Reflection: You Can't Visit Me Where I Live   47

IV.   **Accepting: The New Normal**   49
      My Story: It's All in How You Look at It   50
      Love Him Up   52
      The Resolute Advocate   53
      When the Student Is Ready, the Teacher Will Appear   55
      Respect   57
      Reflection: You Can't Answer Anyone Else's Heart Issues   59

V.   **Renewed: Places to Refuel**   61
      My Story: Seal Skin Soul Skin   62
      Ask, Accept and Enjoy   64
      Find Your Rock in the Sun   66
      The Ring   68
      Knots   70
      Reflection: Faith—To Believe or Not to Believe;
          That Is the Question   72

VI.   **Unexpected Gifts: There Is a Pony in There**   75
      My Story: A Sad Story and a Bad Joke   76
      I Wouldn't Have Missed It for the World   78
      I Like the Way He Looks at Me   80
      The Gift of Closure   81
      The Head of the AWOA   82
      Hindsight Is 20/20   83
      Reflection: Vocation—Discovering a New Path   85

VII. **Epilogue: The Blessing of the Saints**   87

VIII. **A Guide for Friends of Caregivers**   91

Acknowledgments   95

About the Cover Art   99

INTRODUCTION

I remember the day I started my caregiving journey. I was sitting in a neurologist's waiting room with my husband, Gerry, who was having medical problems. One was "frozen shoulder": Gerry's right arm was stiff and no longer had the range of movement it used to have. Gerry's right hand was "frozen," too, in a fist that would not open or even relax. This, of course, was affecting his ability to write; I could hardly recognize his handwriting any more.

Watching Gerry walk down the street with the dog one day, I noticed that he wasn't swinging his right arm and his steps seemed short and tentative. Another day I came home and found him hunched over the computer trying to work. He looked tired and miserable, and he told me that he felt unable to connect his thoughts or to accomplish much of anything. Something was wrong.

We tried various physical therapies for these problems, but nothing worked. One by one, all the different specialists failed to solve the riddle of Gerry's problems. Finally, we ended up in neurology as our last hope for an answer. But even then I was in denial about what was coming. I still thought we would get an answer, a cure. With the neurologist we were going to find out what we needed to do to "fix" Gerry so that we could get on with our life plan.

When the doctor said that my husband had Parkinson's disease, it was my body that reacted first. I felt like I had been socked in the stomach. Suddenly I was weak, defenseless, unable to take a breath. Somehow, my body knew how dire this prognosis was way before my mind could comprehend the words that were being delivered by the doctor.

During the rest of the day, the doctor's words kept coming back to me a few at a time. *Parkinson's disease. No cure. Will get worse. Drugs have side effects. He won't be able to care for himself. Other complications.*

1

My mind could only take in and process the doctor's message piece-meal. I was numb with shock.

And this was just the beginning. As the years passed, I would be forced to come to terms with all the consequences of a chronic disease. Parkinson's was going to rob Gerry of his physical and mental health. Parkinson's was going to make it difficult for him to get around for many years and finally make it impossible for him to walk at all without aid. As he approached the advanced stage of the disease, his ability to think clearly and to plan would be replaced by forgetfulness, confusion, and frustration. It would become extremely difficult to communicate with Gerry because his voice was too soft to hear.

All of this hit both of us particularly hard because Gerry had always been high-energy. He knew he needed to sleep, but he resented it a bit, too, because it took him away from doing things. A casual observer might label Gerry a workaholic. But work was really play for Gerry—he simply liked to build things and make things happen, and he delighted in taking on difficult and detailed problems. Gerry was/is one of the brightest, most intelligent people I know. Conversations with him were always easy and interesting because Gerry cared about everything around him—world history, politics, economics, people, music, other cultures, you name it.

Gerry was the person everyone else depended on to take charge and make things happen, and he became dependent on others for the simple tasks of life. For me, it was like having another child, one who would only get "younger," not older. One who would become more and more dependent upon me.

My first loss was the loss of my dreams of what my life was going to look like as the years went by. I was on the corporate fast track. Promotions had come easily as my superiors groomed me for more and more responsibility, steering me toward executive management classes and the "right" positions. I became director of marketing for a manufacturing company. As Gerry's condition progressed, I continued to work full time. Someone had to have health insurance and pay the bills. I took less-demanding assignments that were more flexible. I said good-bye to my top-management aspirations.

Another thing I had to accept was that there would be no golden retirement years for us. We had always loved to travel and had been to Asia several times, but there was much more we wanted see in other parts of the world. We had discussed starting a hobby business after our careers wound down, just for the fun of it and to work together. Maybe we would move downtown to a condo so that we could be close to all the cultural activities our city provides. All these hopes had to be abandoned.

Finally, there was the realization that my most important new job was to manage our household on my own. The first step came when my husband had to retire from his job. I became the breadwinner and, for the first time in my life, worked because I had to, not because I wanted to.

I began to pick up more and more responsibility around the house. Bit by bit, all the things that my husband used to do were added to my list. I was the one who had to take out the garbage, feed the dog, make all the meals, shovel the snow, cut the grass, pay the bills . . . all little things, but things that added up to make for a very long day. If anything broke, I had to fix it. If any appointments needed to be made, I had to make them. Once Gerry was unable to complete the taxes, I had to somehow figure those out—a job I really hated.

And the kids, who were finishing college, now looked to me for everything. They needed to get on with their lives and were not around much. They never talked about how they felt watching their father's disease progress. But I know that it was painful for them. One of them didn't like to be seen with Gerry outside the house and seemed to avoid coming home.

Then the need to provide more physical care came. I cut up Gerry's food; I carried on his part of the conversation when we were with others because he lost his voice. I helped him get dressed in the morning. I had to look for all the things he put someplace and couldn't find. I picked him up off the floor when he fell. I helped him get in and out of chairs. I tucked him into bed at night. And the hardest work was still to come.

At one point, I started getting up in the morning to write about my experiences and emotions—the anger and fear, the joy and the gifts. I would just dump whatever I was feeling—confusion, guilt, anger, joy, hope—onto a piece of paper. Then I was able to move on with the day. Soon I figured out that I probably wasn't alone with all these confusing feelings. I started to talk to other caregivers and found out they were going through a lot of the same experiences and were just as confused as I was about what they were feeling. In some cases, their stories validated my own reactions. I didn't feel so crazy or lonely after talking to them. In other cases, it was like getting another piece of the puzzle, another clue as to how to move forward with a little more sanity and grace. I began to write these stories down, and this book is the result.

This is not a self-help book or a guide to the nuts and bolts of being a caregiver. There are many books and other resources that can give you all the practical, day-to-day help you need. This book is a collection of stories people have shared about their caregiving experiences—the hard stuff, the funny stories, and the life lessons they have learned along the way. This book is about emotions and their power. It is intended to be a companion for you as you experience the overpowering, confusing feelings that come with caregiving.

This was not a journey I chose. It is a journey very few volunteer for. It's hard. Whether we like it or not, when our partner or another family member for whom we're responsible has a chronic disease like Parkinson's, our lives get redefined. The disease alters the caregiver's life as fundamentally as it alters the life of the person with the diagnosis. As caregivers, our grief over the things that the disease takes away from us—dreams of a future, the freedom to come and go as we please, the energy to pursue a passion—this grief is as real as our partners' feelings about facing a devastating illness.

Caregiving can seem choiceless. Very few of us feel that we have the option of leaving our relationship with the sufferer; most of us feel bound to accept the role of caregiver, in whatever form it takes. But we have an important choice, a defining choice: how we move through the experience and how we come out in the end.

I won't lie to you. Caring for someone with a chronic illness is not fun. The process is painful, and to do it well takes more courage than you probably think you have. But if you refuse to face the challenge, if you fight the reality of the situation and deny what is, the result will be anger, depression, and sadness.

Many of us caregivers do surrender to the reality and rise to the occasion. We have come out of the experience more deeply human, loving, and compassionate. We've discovered what makes life important to ourselves and to our spouses. We've received gifts that we never could have expected.

Many have taken this trip before you. Here are their stories so that you don't feel so alone—and so that you can get a glimpse of those gifts at the other end.

I.

ANGRY

I DIDN'T VOLUNTEER FOR THIS!

MY STORY

This Is Not the Deal I Signed Up For

As my husband's Parkinson's disease progressed, I assumed more and more responsibility. When his hands could no longer write or cut up his own food, I did everything that needed small finger dexterity. When he fell, I made sure that nothing was broken, and if it was, I took him to the hospital emergency room. I helped him get dressed in the morning. I opened up the cans and fed the dog. I paid the bills. When his voice started to fail, I made the phone calls and appointments. I ordered his food at restaurants. I structured conversations with him so he only needed to say yes or no. When his memory started to fail, I found the canes and keys that were lost. I cancelled the credit cards that were no longer in his wallet. And finally, I had to take on responsibility for taxes, a job I truly hated and was ill equipped to do.

I am not proud of how angry I was when I realized what the implications of my husband's illness were to me. I got very angry.

We were a team. We were a successful couple with two great careers and two great kids. We had worked hard and were to reap the benefits of all that effort. If someone had asked me why I married my husband, other than the obvious "I love him," I would have told him or her how interesting and exciting it was to be around him.

We had struck a deal. First, he was going to start his own company with the financial stability my job provided. Then it was going to be my turn. I was going to do something that I loved to do and didn't have to worry about bringing in a paycheck. And besides, he was supposed to be the primary breadwinner who was to take care of me. He reneged on our deal, and I was angry!

As my husband declined, things were taken away from me. I lost my partner. He no longer had the strength to explore things with me for any length of time. Any event had to be planned in great detail and in between naps. I lost my personal time. He could no longer take on his share of responsibility for home and children.

Gradually, I lost freedom. I lost choices about what job assignments I could accept because I could not travel anymore. I had to work at a job I did not like for the salary and healthcare benefits. I wasn't free to pursue my career or other interests that required more time and energy than I had left. I couldn't take off on a trip with friends without making sure everything was in place. And if I did venture out, it was not without preplanning or guilt. I got angry because I was losing the life that I had worked so hard to get.

I got angry with friends who had no idea of what my life was like—and what it was going to be going forward. They made insensitive comments about how hard it must be for my husband, while they totally ignored the impact of Parkinson's on me. They told stories of the long lost sister of their grandmother who had Parkinson's and lived in a nursing home, a relative that they visited once a year. And they would conclude their "sharing" with the description of their latest vacation wind surfing in Hawaii. I would just smile and make an excuse to leave before I said what I really thought.

I lost my dreams for the future. I got angry at the commercials on television that showed older couples walking on the beach holding hands and enjoying their retirement. I knew my future was getting my husband dressed in the morning and administering his drugs multiple times a day.

I was angry because I was losing everything—and it wasn't even my disease.

The Ventriloquist's Dummy

Jane accompanied her husband, Allen, to his regularly scheduled appointment with the neurologist. There's a normal routine to this appointment: First, the nurses take Allen's blood pressure, height, and weight. They check and double-check his medications and ask whether he's taking them as prescribed. The doctor observes Allen walking and his hand movements. If there are scrapes on Allen's knuckles or forehead, there are questions about whether he's fallen. There are questions about swallowing and Allen's daily habits.

The reason Jane goes along to this regular appointment is that Allen can't talk above a whisper. The doctor and the nurses look at Allen as they ask their questions. Allen whispers the answers. Then the nurse and doctor look to Jane to tell them what her husband just said.

Jane has become a ventriloquist's dummy. But her sense of nonentity doesn't stop there.

"At the last appointment the doctor gave my husband a status report," she told me. "The only other thing that the science of medicine can do for my husband is to fine-tune the balance between the deep-brain-stimulation current they send into his brain and the amount and timing of his drugs. The doctor said that my husband should not put off anything he wants to do. He should take that dream trip while he's still mobile. He should say what he wants to say to those around him.

"'No one knows when or if they will walk out into the street and get run over by a bus,' said the doctor. 'But you have more information than most people do about the way your life will evolve. So get on with it.'

"On one hand I agreed with the doctor and was glad that he was saying these things," said Jane. "My husband needs to hear these things from an objective expert who knows the situation. The advice was sound and good."

But then she sighed and added, "What I noticed is that the doctor didn't look at me when he was talking. And he didn't set out the same set of considerations for me. What was I supposed to do with the next few years of *my* life? What should I be doing before more restrictions born of my husband's illness settle in on me? What choices do I have as things progress? I was angry that I was being left out of the equation.

"As the doctor stood up to leave, he touched my arm as if to say, 'I know.' He had very little to give to my husband, and nothing to give to me. But at least the touch acknowledged that I was there."

They Don't Have a Clue

Few people really understand what it's like to be a caregiver, day in and day out, month after month, year after year. How could they understand the kind of support a caregiver needs?

I met Anne for a cup of coffee at a neighborhood bakery. I was amazed at the energy and strength that emanated from her. Here was a woman who was the caregiver of her eighty-year-old husband, who had Parkinson's disease and chronic back pain. Anne described the preceding two months as "exhausting." She had just managed her way through her husband's fall and subsequent stays in the hospital—not once but twice. "Exhausting" was simply a statement of fact for Anne, not a call for self-pity or even empathy.

Anne had been a professional woman for eighteen years. She knew what it was like to be out in the world. She belonged to two professional women's study groups that were made up of women from all walks of life. As Anne's friends passed away or stopped coming around for health reasons, she found other women to socialize with and enjoy.

Then came a situation at church one Sunday morning. Anne and her husband arrived just as the service was starting. She walked in beside her husband, who was riding in on his electric chair. The couple always sat in the same place at the back of the church, but this Sunday their spot had been taken by someone else. Anne's husband insisted on sitting where they always sat. Anne raised her voice when she explained to her husband that it wasn't possible to sit where he wanted, that the service was starting and they had to sit down. She noticed a friend raise an eyebrow.

"I'm supposed to be sweet and kind all the time," said Anne. "But people who expect that don't have a clue! As a caregiver, you've already given so much. No one sees the daily grind. It can make you crabby—and people don't understand.

"Even the doctors don't really understand," she continued. "One doctor told me to make sure my husband doesn't ever fall again. How am I supposed to do that? I'm already with him almost twenty-four hours a day and I can't keep him from falling. It just isn't possible."

I asked Anne what she *did* want from her friends.

"Simple things," she said. "Call me every once in awhile. Don't make me call you when I need support. Stop by and bring us some small food item. Invite me over for dinner. Come see that everything is all right at my house. Send a card, but not a sappy or expensive one. Don't treat me like I'm abnormal. Sometimes when we go out, I feel that people look at us as if we're some kind of spectacle.

"Everyone says, 'Let me know what I can do to help.' That's not helpful to me. That puts the responsibility of asking for help back on me. Just help! I don't need more things to be responsible for.

"I know that most people can't really understand what my life is like. But you can show me that you remember I'm still here."

I Swear Like a Sailor

It was the first time I saw a caregiver shed tears of anger. Cindy was sharing her experience with Parkinson's with our support group. She was mad, fed up, and exhausted. She said, "My husband has had Parkinson's for more than fifteen years. My life sucks. I have no life.

"First, Parkinson's took away my social life. Who wants to go out to eat with my husband when he can't hold a spoon without shaking? He misses his mouth and a good part of his meal ends up on his shirt. No one wants to go out with me.

At first, my friends were empathetic and supportive. But as the years went by and the Parkinson's got worse, most of them faded away. I don't blame them. They couldn't understand my life. After a while, who wanted to hear about how exhausted I was and the list of new things I had to take on? Who wanted to hear about the difficulty of dressing my husband in the morning or the challenge of helping him go to the restroom when I was out in public with him? I know that having a conversation with me is depressing. One old friend asked me when I was going to be *fun* again. But I can no longer lie about how I am doing and say things are just fine."

She continued: "The next thing Parkinson's took away from me was my job. While I was working, at least I had a place to go every day that had nothing to do with the disease. I could pretend for a few hours that it didn't exist. But eventually my health started to deteriorate under the pressure of a full-time job plus caregiving. My husband went to a day program so I could work. But I still had to dress and feed him, get the medications ready, make sure that transportation was arranged, and make sure he got on the bus. After he came home, I had to take care of him until he went to bed and hope that he didn't wake up in the middle of the night, think it was time to get up, and take a shower.

"My employer was patient at first. But as time went on, I missed more and more meetings and deadlines because of doctor appointments or visits to the emergency room. My manager grew impatient and couldn't cover for me any longer. So my job was 'eliminated,' and

I was laid off. It was a relief in some ways. I felt bad that I was always distracted and not fully productive at my job. Now, at least, I was down to one job.

"When my husband's dementia set in, it wasn't safe to leave him alone. Yesterday he tried to ride his bicycle to his friend's house—on the freeway. After a while, it became easier just to stay at home with him than to find and manage outside help or ask my kids.

"I can't take a walk or go shopping by myself. If I could get some exercise, maybe I could get a good night's sleep.

"My final loss is that Parkinson's has taken my husband. He is gone. He is physically here. But he can no longer do anything on his own. He's like a toddler who needs constant help and supervision—and he wants what he wants *now*. My husband is no longer my partner and support. I used to depend on him to listen to me, understand me, and help me through challenging times. We used to have fun going places and doing things. We used to be able to have interesting conversations over a meal. My husband is no longer here.

"I am getting screwed. I have lost my life and my husband—and I still have more years of Parkinson's to face. All I can do is go into the closet and scream. I hope my husband doesn't hear me swear like a sailor out of frustration. It's not his fault, and I don't want to take it out on him."

The support group sat and listened. They understood. They were going through similar experiences . . . or knew that they would be soon. At least Cindy had the group, a time and place where it was safe to tell the truth and vent her emotions. That helped her go home and face another day.

Sati—The Burning of the Widow

Julie had traveled the world and learned about many different cultures. When we got together for coffee, she told me about a Hindu custom called *sati* (which, thankfully, is no longer legal or practiced). Sati is believed to be a voluntary act in which a woman decides to join her husband in death. The widow is burnt to ashes on her dead husband's funeral pyre. For some Hindus, this practice is the epitome of wifely devotion and promotes the salvation of the dead husband.

In the United States, people react with horror to this practice; it violates what we see as the right of the individual to pursue happiness and a fulfilled life. It doesn't make sense to us that just because one person dies, another must. For those who believe in equal rights for women, this custom seems the ultimate violation; after all, the husband is not expected to sacrifice himself at his wife's death.

Julie said to me, "I am coming to the conclusion that there are some things that are similar to sati in our society. They're just more subtle.

"When I started sharing with others that my husband had Parkinson's disease," she went on, "people made comments that caught me off guard: 'How long will you be able to work before you have to quit and stay home to take care of your husband?' 'Of course, you are going to do everything you can to keep your husband at home as long as possible, so that he doesn't have to go to a nursing home.' All these comments carried an underlying assumption—that my life was to be sacrificed for the care of my husband, no matter what the personal cost to me.

"I started down that path. Of course, I would have to quit my job in a few years to stay at home and take care of my husband. Of course, I would be his caregiver until I could no longer physically manage it. Of course, I would stop pursuing my passions and interests so that I could spend as much time as possible with him. The only thing these assumptions produced was anger . . . and then depression. I felt trapped and believed I no longer had any options. I was going to have to sacrifice my hopes and dreams to take care of my husband. It wasn't fair!

"Would sacrificing everything that is important in my life make my husband's illness go away? Is his life better if I am either angry with him or depressed all the time? Can I provide better care for him if I give up things that nourish me? Can I give him back his health by sacrificing my life?"

Julie concluded our conversation this way: "This life experience has forced me to examine what is really important to me. I've discovered the things that are so essential to my life-spirit that I have to hold on to them no matter what. I am discovering that the things that other people told me were important, are not. I have found that even though I am willing to get off the 'fast track' at work, I still need to have a place to be productive, be a part of a community, and be rewarded for my skills. I have found that I need to work at something . . . even if it's smaller than what I do today. Being angry at the world for having to sacrifice myself for my husband isn't the answer. I can't follow the American version of sati."

For the sake of her sanity, Julie put her husband in a day program Monday through Friday so that she could continue to work. A companion was hired to come and be with her husband Saturday afternoon so Julie could run errands and have a little time for herself. Early mornings were still hard—she had to get him ready to go to the day program. When he got home, her evening duty began: she took care of him until he went to bed. It seemed like she was tired all the time. But Julie was keeping parts of her life intact and her life was not consumed by Parkinson's twenty-four hours a day.

Last Christmas Julie's husband had seizures, and the result was a significant decrease in his cognitive abilities. He didn't know what day it was, and if told, he couldn't remember the information a half hour later. When he dressed himself, he chose clothes that were inappropriate for the weather and sometimes put them on backwards. If there were an emergency, Julie's husband wouldn't be able to figure out what to do. He could no longer be left alone.

For the sake of her soul she continued her arts pursuits and seeing her friends. Even though it would have been easy for her to decide that she had no time for these things, she was fierce in her determination to make time for them. On Saturdays, she brought in a companion to help with her husband so she had three hours to spend outside of the house. She made sure that she regularly had lunch or a cup of coffee with people who gave her energy. Julie kept doing her art, even if she could only manage half an hour late at night when she was tired. It gave her enough energy to handle another day.

"I don't know how long I can do this," she said to me. "But I have clearly identified the things I cannot do. I cannot be a full-time nurse if he falls or gets seriously hurt. I cannot take care of him when he has to eat through a feeding tube. I cannot take care of him when dementia takes him to a different world. Basically, when I cannot work and have to be a caregiver and nurse twenty-four hours a day, I will need to put him in assisted living or another care facility.

"Although I deeply love my husband, I am starting to realize that he is no longer the husband I once had. In many ways, I've lost him already. It tears me up inside to realize that and to know he will eventually need to go live someplace else . . . but that time will come."

Two Strikes, But She's Not Out

Nora admitted she almost called and cancelled our lunch. Why should she get together with another caregiver she didn't know and talk about her "story"? What could I know about her situation? She was right.

Nora had a double load to carry. Nora was caregiver to her husband who had been diagnosed with neuropathy ten years ago AND Nora had Parkinson's herself. Nora was both the caregiver and the person with the chronic condition. And guess what, Nora was angry. "I have been robbed of my health. My husband's illness has robbed me of things that I want to do with the time I have left! This is not what retirement was supposed to be."

Nora's husband was no longer the person she had married. Nora didn't expect much from her husband given his medical condition. But he didn't even try. "I can't depend on him to take out the garbage," she said. Once he was a compassionate, charismatic person who could make anyone feel at ease. Now he just sits in the apartment and doesn't want to leave to go play cards with his friends like he used to. By choosing to isolate himself, he had trapped Nora in the apartment with him. Nora's husband didn't even bother to ask Nora how she was doing. "He's no longer my husband or partner. It is hard to feel so responsible and so alone."

Several things amazed me about Nora. First, the burden of taking care of her husband was harder on her than the burden of her own Parkinson's. Other than describing some physical symptoms that kept her from doing some of the things she had always done, Nora talked little about her own health. The thing that affected her life the most was her husband's condition. It had taken so much away from her, much more than her own illness.

The second thing that was amazing about Nora was that she had not given up. Her spirit was strong. She did not ask for pity. She could clearly see how her circumstances affected her. She saw that life had stacked the game against her, and she didn't like it. In fact, she was angry and wanted to change what she could still change.

I asked Nora what she would be doing if things were different. What would she be doing if her husband wasn't chronically ill or if she was on her own? Nora did not hesitate to answer. "Travel would be the first thing I would do." Nora described a walking tour of England she had gone on by herself with Elder Hostel. Australia was the next place on her list of places to visit. "I would write. Did you know I am a published writer?" she said with a broad smile on her face. "I wrote an article for my writing class, and it was published in a regional newspaper. I would go to the theater, and I would take an art history class. And I just want some time to myself in the apartment."

"Parkinson's doesn't define me," Nora said. "I am still Nora, and I want to be happy again. I am seventy years old, and I don't have a lot of years left."

Nora had been robbed of her health and independence. She had a right to be angry. But the anger showed that life had not taken her spirit away from her. She was going to fight for what little she could get. Life had two strikes against her, and it was the bottom of the ninth inning. But the game was not over yet for Nora. She was angry, and she was a fighter.

REFLECTION

Moses Deserved to Go to the Promised Land, Didn't He?

Americans live in a world of cause and effect. Science, which we believe in, is based on observing cause and effect and then using the relationship to predict outcomes. Engineering and physics take this analytical discipline and construct a world based on materials and principles that have been tested. Our world is made up of construction, transportation, electricity, electronics, and many other systems based on scientific evidence.

Medicine follows the same process. If we can test the different aspects of the body to find out what prevents illness, we can lay out guidelines for a healthy life. If we test the body for the abnormalities called disease, we can identify the problems and fix them. We can cure people.

We take this belief in cause and effect and apply it to the rest of our lives as well. If we go to college, we will have a better job. If we work hard, we'll be successful. If we marry the "right" person, we will have a happy marriage. If we are good parents, we'll have good kids. If we eat right and exercise, we'll be healthy.

So what happens when we do all the "right" things, and we don't get the "right" results? What happens when we work hard and don't get what we deserve? How do we feel when God and Life renege on the "deal"? What happens when something terrible happens to us (or a loved one) that should not have happened? We cry out, "Why me, Lord?"

For me, and I daresay many others, it means anger . . . and a lot of it. It means being angry at an unfair world. It means being angry with the person who is sick and who is now an added responsibility. It means being angry with the people around me who are doing well and whom life is treating "fairly." It means being angry at God.

But when did God sign the piece of paper saying that if I was good, I would get everything I think I deserve? Did God ever say He would do things my way? Did God ever say that I should get everything I want? I keep trying to cut a deal with my God . . . a deal that God doesn't recognize.

What comes to my mind when I think about these things is the story of Exodus. The Israelites tried to do the same thing we do. They couldn't figure out why they, as God's chosen people, had to serve as the slaves of the Egyptians. When they did escape, they wanted assurances that they would be transported to their promised land quickly and easily. When they did not get what they expected, they tried to find another god who would do what they wanted. So God made the Israelites wander in the desert for a long time until they finally accepted the fact that they were not in control.

The "kicker" to the story is that the one person who did all that he was asked to do didn't get to enter the Promised Land. Moses, sometimes reluctantly, did what God asked. He never tried to find another god who would do things his way. If anyone deserved to see the Promised Land, it was Moses. (There are a few passages in Numbers and Deuteronomy where God tells Moses that he "broke faith" with Him in the wilderness of Zin. But it seems to me that forty years of faithful service to God outweighs one incident with a rock at Zin!) So why didn't Moses get what he deserved? Why was he stopped and allowed only to look at the place he spent forty years traveling toward?

I believe the answer is that God commissioned Moses to do a job. Moses accomplished the task—and that was it. It ended before the entry into the Promised Land.

Unfair? Maybe. But "fair" is a concept we have thought up. To believe that God needs to be fair is to believe in a god that we have created out of our belief in cause and effect. To believe that we should get what we want and deserve is to believe we can take control away from God and make the world work the way we want it to.

Not only is this a form of idolatry; it also prevents us from receiving God's grace. Oftentimes we get much more than we deserve. Oftentimes we get gifts from God that are much greater than we could have ever imagined. If we spend all of our time being angry about not getting what we're sure we deserve, we miss seeing what we are getting that we didn't earn.

And after all, Moses did get more than he deserved. His relationship with God was more intimate than he would have been capable of on his own. God helped Moses accomplish the task of leading the Israelites out of Egypt in miraculous ways. God never deserted Moses during all those years of hardships. He saw the final accomplishment of his holy commission. He was close to God at the top of the mountain as he looked over the Promised Land.

I didn't get what I wanted or deserved when my husband got Parkinson's at such an early age. I had all the emotions that came with that—disbelief, depression, and plenty of anger. And at any point in time, good or bad, I would have paid anything to make my husband well, to get back to our lives as they once were.

But on this journey, I did learn some important life lessons, and some incredible gifts came my way once I dealt with my anger.

Thank goodness God is gracious and gives us more than we deserve, even if it's hard to see and accept that fact sometimes. And thank goodness God can handle my anger—and doesn't get angry back.

II.

SCARED

THE GREAT UNKNOWN

MY STORY

Control—My Favorite Form of Denial

My favorite form of denial was to believe that if I learned enough about what was going to happen, laid out the timelines, and made sure that every contingency plan was in place, I could control what Parkinson's was going to do to my husband, to me, and to us. If I could control the Parkinson's, I could control the terrifying fear that came over me like a tidal wave threatening to drown me.

My world at the time that Parkinson's disease came into our lives was the business world. I was well taught by that world that there is nothing that cannot be achieved, controlled, or overcome. You first identified the goal. Without out a goal, you just wander. Once the goal is clear, you gather data and information to help you figure out the steps involved in achieving the identified goal. You assess the resources needed. You lay out a timeline. And, heaven forbid things don't go as planned, you lay out the contingency plan.

Every time we made a visit to the neurologist, I would ask the question, "How long . . . ? Where are we in the process? What happens next?" We would meet with the social worker at the Parkinson's center every six months to evaluate my husband's capabilities to maintain a "normal" life. I made sure that I knew where the resources were in case of an emergency or bad turn of events. I got our wills and estates in order. I knew what our financial situation was and what our retirement income would be depending on how many years I could continue to work.

I would spend hours planning in my head. My internal dialogue was taken over by all the "ifs and thens" that made up my plan. If my husband can stay independent for X number of years . . . If I can continue my job for X number of years . . . If our kids live at home (or at least lived close by) . . . If I engineer the house to be more accessible . . . then everything would be okay.

But it wasn't okay. I wasn't okay.

As I sat talking to Cathy, I had to admit that I was exhausted. My body was falling apart. My jaw ached because I was thrusting it forward all the time in determination. My neck wouldn't turn all the way to the side because my muscles were so tight. My leg went numb from time to time because my posture was poor and my lower back was strained. I was feeling anxious and unsettled. I had done what I should do, planned for all possibilities. But all this planning was draining me of energy. And when I got done planning the same thing over and over, I was still terrified of what I knew was coming.

Then Cathy said, "You will know when the time comes." She proceeded to tell me the experience that she and her family had gone through with one parent who had Parkinson's and the other who had Alzheimer's. At each step of the way, it become clear that the situation had shifted and that a new step needed to be taken. It happened with an event. It happened with the acknowledgment that things were not working anymore. It happened with a fall. It happened when a recovery did not follow.

What Cathy was telling me was that fear was not a helpful emotion to be stuck in. Planning for events that are likely is a good thing. But living in perpetual fear was taking its toll. All the contingency planning I was doing over and over was taking energy, and it was not going to change the future. What Cathy was telling me was to stop wasting my precious energy worrying about the future that wasn't here yet.

Cathy was telling me that I will know what to do each time a change comes. I can't plan my way out of the inevitable. I can't prevent each struggle that will come regardless. I can't make my husband well. I can't keep him safe from everything. But at each turn, I will know what to do. With each change of circumstances, I will have the capacity to deal with it at that time.

What Cathy was telling me was to accept the present moment—both its struggle and joy.

The Great Unknown

Joan and I met at a restaurant. I walked in not knowing what to expect. What would this person be like? Was her husband further down the Parkinson's path than my husband? What weighed on Joan as she dealt with the same illness that I was dealing with?

Joan was young, only fifty-two years old. She had married an "older man" now in his seventies. He had been diagnosed with Parkinson's disease six years earlier. That meant that Joan's husband was still functioning relatively independently. But the reality of what Parkinson's was going to bring was starting to appear on a regular basis. There was difficulty walking, some forgetfulness, some impulsiveness, and the Parkinson's face.

Joan struck me as a capable person. She had held a responsible corporate job until recently. She sought out resources for herself as well as her husband. She maintained a strong set of friends she could enjoy and with whom she could vent when that was necessary. From an outside perspective, Joan seemed to be managing a tough situation very well. In fact, she was a survivor of brain surgery and breast cancer. Joan knew how to get through rough times.

But as we talked more, it was apparent that this confident, capable woman was scared. The questions tumbled out of her. She hoped that I could help her figure out how to deal with what Parkinson's was doing to her husband.

Where was my husband in the process?
Did we have long-term healthcare insurance?
Did my husband nod off at times during the day?
Did he sleep well at night?
How often did my husband fall?
Did my husband forget things like his keys?
Could my husband still drive?
Who was taking care of our finances?

And as Joan and I compared details of our situations, I realized how scary this journey is.

No one can predict the future or prevent things from happening. But most people are able to tuck any questions and fears into the back of their minds and move through the day, taking it as it comes.

But when your loved one has a chronic condition, life takes on a different dynamic. It is scary. You know that the illness is only going to get worse. The fear can no longer be tucked away after a certain point. How many times will my husband fall today? How many times will he forget something at the store before it is something important? How fast will things progress? What will I do when this or that happens? These questions and more present themselves when you notice what the disease is doing to your loved only on a daily basis. The questions that Joan was asking me came from a deep fear of what was coming.

Toward the end of our conversation, Joan said, "In a cosmic sense, I've been chosen to do this. And God will give me what I need. And if that's not true, I am going to be pissed." Then Joan told a story about the weekend after her husband's Parkinson's had been confirmed and she had learned that she had breast cancer. They had headed to church in the lake community they visited on weekends when they went to the cabin. Joan and her husband had come late for the first service and decided to stick around and be early for the second service. Before the second service began, they ran into a couple with whom they were acquaintances. As the four of them were talking, Joan and her husband found out that the other gentleman had just been diagnosed with Parkinson's and that the woman had just gone through surgery for breast cancer. In fact, Joan and the woman had the same surgeon.

Joan finished telling this story by saying, "No one can tell me that there isn't a God. God put those people there because that is who we needed to be with at that moment. I found people who understood the fear I was feeling. I at least had company on the journey."

Joan has found a way to deal with the "scariness" of her life. "There are good days and bad days. I vent and swear." Joan also asks for the help she needs, and receives it when she needs it.

The Real Question

Laura signed up for an annual conference on Parkinson's disease. One day a year the experts in Parkinson's disease gathered interested parties together at a hotel to discuss the latest research and advice about the disease. The ballroom was full of strangers connected by one thing— Parkinson's. About half of the attendees had the disease, and the other half were care partners. The impressive panel of experts was seated on the stage at the front of the room. The stage and all the letters behind their job titles elevated them above the rest of the room.

Laura was scared to ask her question in front of a ballroom full of people. What if they didn't understand her question or thought it was stupid? She kept reminding herself that the people in the room were like her. They were all trying to cope with this thing called Parkinson's, whether they were the person with the disease or the person who had assumed the role of care partner.

Laura raised her hand and was handed the microphone. Her knees were weak as she stood up to speak. Laura spoke from the heart. Her six-foot father had Parkinson's and now needed help to get up from a chair or get in and out of bed. Her petite mother could no longer handle this physical task by herself, so Laura was trying to help out as much as possible. She was coming in before work to help get her father dressed and coming back in the evening so that she and her mother could get her father into bed.

What help or advice could these esteemed experts give Laura and her mother? Where could she turn as the physical demands of taking care of her father increased and eventually became overwhelming? Laura was afraid she and her mother couldn't take much more. That she and her mother couldn't handle what she knew the future was going to bring.

The answers that Laura got that day were fairly straightforward. There was special furniture that would make the situation easier. Certain chairs and beds were easier to get in and out of. When that was no longer enough, someone could come and assess the house for rails, bars, and ramps that would make the rooms more accessible. Physical therapy had exercises and tricks her father could do that would strengthen his body and keep him as independent as possible for as long as possible. When the time came, trained professionals could come into their home to help get Laura's father bathed, dressed, and settled for the day. These people could come back in the evening to do the reverse. If resources were an issue, there were funds and volunteers available to help out. Everyone on the panel had seen this scenario before and wanted to be as helpful and supportive as possible.

But the real question that Laura was asking was how were Laura and her mother going to survive her father's Parkinson's—physically AND emotionally? The experts didn't hear the question . . . or didn't have an answer. For the panel, Parkinson's was a disease that, if not curable, was to be managed. They had tools that they enlisted to do this—drugs, therapies, and deep-brain stimulation. The goal of these professionals is to keep the symptoms at bay for the person who has the disease. Their goal is to help with the quality of life for the person with Parkinson's. That is what they do.

As Laura sat down, the other question, maybe the real question was never answered. How were Laura and her mother going to survive the "heavy lifting" that came with caring for Laura's father? There was the heavy lifting involved in facing the facts. The fact of a spouse and father who was becoming more and more dependent on them, not only for daily care, but mental and emotional help as well. The fact that Laura's and her mother's days were being consumed by the management of another person's life. The fact that Laura and her mother were watching their loved one drift away from them bit by bit. As Parkinson's consumed more and more of Laura's father, the lifting was heavier than the weight of his body.

Laura would have to look elsewhere for her answer. Maybe it would come from within. Maybe it would come from care partners who had already traveled the same road. Maybe it would come from Laura's deep faith and daily prayers. Laura would just need to keep asking, and have faith that the answer would come.

Where's the Hope?

I met Emily at her art studio. She was seven years into her journey with her husband's Parkinson's disease. And Parkinson's was only one of the many "hits" that Emily had experienced in the past few years. Emily had watched her mother die of congestive heart disease. Her husband's mother had died of lung cancer. Her friend Bill had passed away. Her husband, Jack, had lost his business, and they had had to file for bankruptcy. Her kids had grown and left home. The losses for Emily were piling up.

Even though Emily was pretty good at living in the present, she couldn't help asking questions about how the future was going to look. When Jack started shaking more and dropping things, the questions surfaced. When her super-responsible husband started forgetting things, the questions would come again. How much longer before Parkinson's moved into their lives, robbing her husband of his health and quality of life?

How was she going to take care of Jack with few financial resources? When her friends were talking about retiring and taking trips, Emily was trying to figure out how to make a little more money as an artist, the occupation for which she had been trained. And she did not like thinking about the additional caretaking responsibilities and tasks that were coming her way. How much longer before Parkinson's would steal Emily's independence and her dreams?

The image of fear that Emily carried around with her was of being underwater in a cave. Every once in a while she would be able to swim to the surface to take a breath of fresh air. Then she would have to go back down to her cave underwater, where she couldn't breathe. It was no surprise to her that she suffered from asthma and had a hard time sleeping.

Several times in our conversation, Emily asked, "Where's the hope?" Her eyes were tired, sad, and full of fear. I could sense her pain from the questions she did not want to ask . . . and the answers she did not want to hear. She knew what was ahead and feared there was no hope for her.

But as Emily continued to talk, I realized that she had answered her own question in a meaningful way.

Part of the answer hung on the walls of her studio. In these paintings, Emily pictured women who had suffered. There were pictures of women who had struggled and suffered on the prairies of the Midwest. There was a picture of a woman who had been taken away to a mental institution when she could no longer cope with the demands of life. There was a picture of a thirteen-year-old girl who was stoned to death after having been raped by soldiers.

The other powerful image in each of the paintings was the Ouroboros. This is an image of a snake eating itself. It represents eternity, the continuity of life, and the totality of the universe. It's the primordial symbol of creation. This circle surrounded the suffering and symbolized death, transformation, and the rebirth of life. Emily portrayed suffering in these works, but the Ouroboros showed that there is something bigger and more powerful in life than suffering.

Then Emily showed me some of the products of the vision mapping that she had been practicing for eleven years. (Vision mapping is a practice in which you collage together pictures cut from magazines or other sources to describe your life, honor your values, and discover the path forward. Emily called it "sacred facilitation of life.")

She showed me a vision map that she had done eleven years earlier. It had pictures of large tables, a studio, a piece of luggage, an easel, and drawing models. At that time in her life Emily did not know what all these images meant—but what they meant, of course, was that she longed to have the facilities and the identity of a serious artist. At the time, she had no means by which to make that happen. But there she was, eleven years later, in her studio with exactly the easel that was in her picture, an easel given to her by a friend. We were standing at two large tables with art materials spread out. She had taken art classes, developed a decorative-painting business, and traveled.

Emily's answer to her question "Where's the hope?" was inside Emily. She just needed to create a vision and let it happen. For a Parkinson's partner, the fear does not go away, but there are openings, and there is hope. For Emily, that opening to hope was there in her art, for all to see.

The Prophet on the Plane

For seven years after her husband was diagnosed with Parkinson's disease, Amy kept going with her life. If she could pretend that nothing needed to change, she could pretend that Parkinson's didn't exist for her and her husband. The fear of what was coming could be pushed into the future. It could be ignored, and Amy could pretend that maybe it wouldn't even happen.

Eventually, Amy became the breadwinner of the family and the provider of healthcare benefits. Her job in sales required that she get on airplanes on a regular basis.

Amy described a particular trip. "It started out like any other trip. I got to the airport, waited in line at security, waited at the gate, climbed on board the plane with my carry-on luggage, and secured my coveted aisle seat. As a frequent flyer, I looked forward to the bit of peace and quiet I got on an airplane. I knew never to make eye contact with the person seated next to me to protect my cocoon.

"As always, this plane was going to be full. I was relieved when a small, older woman with beautiful white hair sat next to me.

"I don't know why I started to talk to her. 'Where are you headed? Why are you going there?' I asked, for some reason. I then found out why she was sitting next to me. She was a prophet sent to me."

The woman was on her way to give a lecture on African art, which she had studied while following her husband around the world for his job. Her husband had recently died after a long struggle with Parkinson's. She had been his caregiver during this illness, even when he was in the nursing home.

Amy continued: "I confessed that my husband had Parkinson's disease too and started to ask her questions. I needed to find out how to handle the painful situation in which I now found myself, a situation I knew was only going to get worse. What did this challenge look like to someone who had traveled the path already? Did she have any advice for me? How did she stay strong? Where did she get help? How did she survive during those years? Was it better or worse now that her husband was gone? Maybe this woman would help quell my fear of what was coming and tell me it wouldn't be that bad."

Amy said, "I didn't like what she told me, which was simple and clear. 'Surrender to it,' she said.

"I didn't follow her advice for years. I kept trying to find the magic formula to keep my life intact and my husband 'well.' Maybe if I ignored the situation, it would go away. Maybe if we got the right drugs, they would make things better. Maybe if he had brain surgery, it would take the symptoms away.

"After all these years I am just starting to understand her words," Amy said. "Surrendering doesn't make the fear go away. But fighting the fear takes so much more energy than living with it and taking it as it comes. Of course, I am afraid. But when I can, I admit that I am afraid. Then it doesn't seem so overwhelming. I can live with that."

REFLECTION

Barking at a Snowman

One night I let our dog, Winston, out before we went to bed. It had snowed earlier that day, so it was cold and I didn't expect Winston to stay out long.

Suddenly I heard him bark. Winston, a quiet, gentle dog, rarely barks. So when he continued to do so, I knew something unusual was going on.

I opened the door to see what was out there. There was Winston, by the door, barking at the snowman that the neighbor's son had made earlier in the day. Winston kept it up until I pulled him back inside the house.

Barking at a snowman seems like a metaphor for how I am living my life these days. How often do I tense up and anticipate things that don't happen and that are not real? How often do I borrow problems from the future long before I really have to deal with them? How many times do I expect the worst, only to find out things somehow work out? I spend much of my time fearing things that probably won't happen.

I have to stop barking at snowmen. I need to live my life one day at a time. I need to have faith that I will figure out the next step when I have to take it. I need to realize that others have traveled this road before me, and have not only survived, but come out stronger, wiser, and more loving.

I know, too, that the snowman will eventually melt when spring arrives.

III.

SAD

WHERE'S THE LIGHT SWITCH? IT'S DARK IN HERE

MY STORY

I Knew I Was in Trouble

I knew I was in trouble as I walked down the hallway to my office. I sat at my desk, looked at my computer, and couldn't figure out what to do next. I didn't know how I was going to get through the day without breaking out screaming, or in tears, when I was supposed to look cheery and confident. All I wanted to do was go home and hide. Then again, I didn't want to go home because there I had even worse problems. My husband's Parkinson's disease was a monster that had invaded our home. I was tired to the bone.

My thoughts, barely rational, were clearly of no value. I fantasized about retiring from my job and doing what I "wanted to do." But my fantasies were nothing more than thoughts of escaping to—what? To something I couldn't figure out or describe. I had made detailed plans, complete with timelines, of how I was going to take care of my husband—only to realize I had no control.

I was trapped and could not find my way out.

Then I found Alice. When I walked into her office and sat on the couch across from her, I explained that I needed some help. "I think I am depressed," I said. After I spent a few minutes describing the circumstances of my life, Alice looked at me with kind eyes and said, "Of course, you are depressed. Why wouldn't you be?"

When Alice went on to explain that my depression was a natural part of grieving, I heaved a deep sigh. When she said that I was grieving not only my husband's physical losses, but the loss of my dreams, the tears began to come. When she told me the pain that I was feeling was okay and wouldn't kill me, my body released some of its defenses. My healing began.

Dealing with my depression took time, and sometimes it comes back for a visit. It's like that relative you don't want around but need to pay attention to—if you ignore her she won't give you any peace.

He Seems All Right to Me

I loved listening to Molly. Her faint Scottish accent was lyrical and matched the twinkle in her eyes. Molly is petite and was impeccably dressed when we met. Looking at her, you can't guess what she has been through in the last ten years.

Molly said that for the first eight years after her husband, Andy, was diagnosed with Parkinson's disease, things were pretty stable. Life was manageable. But in the last two years, things had gone downhill fast. Andy's "freezing" increased, and he was having difficulty walking without a walker. He was hallucinating because of the medications he took and was beginning to drift away from Molly mentally. A few months earlier, when Andy was in the hospital with complications from a virus, the doctors told Molly that she could not care for her husband at home any longer. "It was almost a relief that they forced the issue," Molly said. She was exhausted.

"For the first three weeks, I cried every day for the life we had. I didn't want to meet anyone because I knew I would get upset telling the story of what was happening. I decided to go to a counselor, and that helped a lot.

"Today I don't cry anymore. I still feel sad that our life is like this. But we have to make the best of what we can. I just pray that I won't get sick because it would be hard for Andy to deal with that.

"I intend to keep going to the counselor. I would advise anyone else to do the same."

These days Molly goes back and forth between her apartment and the care center every day to be with Andy. She is balancing her responsibilities at home with the attention that her husband demands. Andy is angry about being in the care center, and he's taking it out on Molly.

Molly talked about how hard it is being a caregiver. One of the most difficult things, she said, is that so few people really understand what it is like to be a caregiver. "They don't get it. They have a conversation with Andy, and he seems okay to them. What they don't see is that my life partner is not the same person he was. They don't see his anger at being at the care center. He complains about the aides, the TV in his room, or something else, every day. They don't see the details that are hard to deal with—that he can't read the clock correctly anymore; that his train of thought gets confused."

Molly continued, "That is just the emotional part. People don't see the physical demands on me either. They don't see all the things I do when I am not with Andy. I have to take care of the apartment, all the bills, all the doctor appointments, and all the paperwork that goes with his care. The list of responsibilities is endless. And then I am supposed to be at the care center every day to be with him."

I asked Molly what she does to take care of herself. The Care Partners Support Group at the Parkinson's Center was her "refuge." "You can say anything you want there because you know they understand," she said. "People come and go, but we are all dealing with the same thing." Molly added that going into the walk-in closet at home and screaming into a pillow is helpful, too.

As I talked to Molly, I realized how lonely the caregiver role is. There are very few people who truly understand what you are going through mentally, emotionally, and physically. Your friends can be supportive . . . and thank goodness for that. But late at night after an exhausting day, it is just you trying to figure out how to make all the pieces fit and how to make it through another day. You are responsible for your life *and* someone else's life in a way that most people do not experience. The person whom you shared a life with is no longer there to share it with you; instead, you are caring for that person, and that person is leaving you, day by day.

"I miss being together," Molly said, as she left to go visit her husband.

The World Gets Smaller

Sherry's shoulders were slumped over as she and her husband walked into their "new place," an assisted living apartment in a retirement center. Changes like this were coming fast, and she couldn't do anything to stop them. If someone had asked her how she was doing with all this change, tears would have come to her eyes. She just wanted things to go back to the way they were.

Her husband of fifty-some years had Parkinson's. His last health scare had put him into the hospital. At some moments during his stay, she was sure he would never come home again. But he *did* come home. His overall condition had deteriorated, however, and it was clear that another crisis could come at any time. He needed more support around him all the time, just in case.

Sherry's husband had, of course, lost his freedom. He couldn't come and go as he wanted. And what had happened to him had happened to Sherry, too. It wasn't just the scare of almost losing someone she loved that was oppressing her. It wasn't just the sadness of seeing him lose another piece of his health. It was the progressive loss of *her* freedom.

Sherry was healthy and still active. She still worked part time. She didn't need the money, but she enjoyed having a place to go where her mind could stay active and where she could contribute, a place where she belonged and was valued for her experience.

Now that was slowly being taken away from her. Every morning Sherry had to make sure that her husband was okay. Had he taken his medications? Was he able to get in and out of the shower without falling? Did he have a doctor's appointment that day? Were there new doctor's appointments to be made? If he wanted to go out, she had to be available.

When Sherry went to work, she made sure she checked in on her husband on a regular basis. She couldn't travel far from home for any reason. Most nights when she got home, he was eager for her company after being alone all day. Sherry's world was getting smaller and smaller all the time, and she didn't see any way back.

The "new place" was part of the answer. The retirement center had a lot of support systems. There were activities that Sherry's husband could take part in; he wouldn't be alone all day. There were healthcare professionals available twenty-four hours a day. There were two dining rooms. All this would give Sherry a little more of her freedom back. She could come and go without worry.

But for the moment, Sherry still held back the tears. She was still going to lose the life she had. She and her husband would move out of the big family home in which they had raised their family. The "new place" in the retirement center was a one-bedroom apartment with a small patio instead of a yard. The rooms were half the size of the ones in their house, so they could only take half their furniture. There was a parking space instead of a garage.

Sherry would lose the garden she planted every summer and her sewing room. She would lose the home office she escaped to when she wanted to be alone with her thoughts. The new place didn't have enough room for the bookshelves that held the treasures they had picked up on their travels around the world.

Sherry's world, like her husband's, was getting smaller. And down deep she knew it would continue to get smaller. Soon her life would be bound by the walls of their apartment, an occasional trip to the grocery store, and the never-ending doctor's appointments. At least she had the mementos from around the world to remind her how big their lives had been at one time.

Which One of Us Is Sick?

I called Elizabeth on the phone. It was her husband's birthday that day. He had died a few months earlier at the age of eighty-two after battling Parkinson's for fifteen years. Elizabeth and Wesley had been married for fifty-six years.

My first thoughts were, "This isn't the best use of my time on this Sunday afternoon." After all, Elizabeth's experience was different from mine. My husband was diagnosed with Parkinson's when he was fifty-four years old . . . and I was only forty-five. Elizabeth's ability to accept the struggle was better because, even though Parkinson's is hard to deal with no matter when it comes, it is also part of growing old. She had had many good years with her husband. Less had been taken away from her.

In fact, much of the conversation reinforced my opinion. Elizabeth expressed no anger or frustration about those fifteen years. She talked in a very matter-of-fact way about that period of time, describing the events that led up to the diagnosis. She described Wesley's first major symptom: difficulty getting his leg over the middle bar of a bicycle. Later she learned that the doctor had suspected Wesley had Parkinson's long before the bicycle incident, but he hadn't mentioned it until several months after it.

When I asked what the hardest part had been for her, her reply put me off a bit. She said that she was an optimist. The process had been gradual. She just took the next step in front of her. "No use in falling apart," she said. Even when she talked about the experience of putting Wesley into a nursing home, she said, "I knew it was for the best. I couldn't take care of him any longer."

But I just needed to keep listening to Elizabeth's story to find out how wrong I was in thinking that Parkinson's hadn't really touched her.

Elizabeth talked about the day she knew she needed to put Wesley into a nursing home. "I had never had anxiety before. I didn't know what was happening to me. Evidently, whatever was wrong had been building up in me. When I woke up that morning—it's still hard to explain—I was full of fear. I told myself 'I can't take care of him if I don't feel good.'

"The thing is, I didn't expect the reason for moving Wesley into a care facility would be me."

Elizabeth was having anxiety attacks. It seemed that others could see what was happening, the toll Wesley's illness was taking on her, before she could. "I remember that my daughter had wanted me to put Wesley in a home earlier," she said. "But I had had enough of her telling me what to do! I guess I hung up on her a couple of times."

Elizabeth summed it up: "I knew that Wesley was deteriorating mentally and physically, but it never occurred to me that *I* would get 'sick' and not be able to care for him."

This is one of several stories I have heard from caregivers who pay a price for all the love and caring they expend on their loved one. More often than not, they pay this price without realizing how costly caregiving is to them. They are too busy or overwhelmed with their role.

My Heart Is Forever Broken,
But I Can Live with That

The first thing that Debbie said to me when we sat down to talk was how touched she was with the story I wrote about a fellow caregiver, Amy, who met a woman on a plane who told her to "surrender" to her husband's illness. As I listened, I learned about Debbie's journey to "surrender."

Debbie's husband, John, had been diagnosed with Parkinson's nine and a half years ago. He had been a dentist with a thriving practice. He was a strong and athletic man who could continue his active life after the diagnosis, with some adjustments.

While in the hospital for deep-brain-stimulation surgery, he had seizures. This was the beginning of significant changes. After five days in the hospital and two weeks in transitional care, John came home. "He wasn't quite the same after that," Debbie said. Now John showed signs of confusion more often. Sometimes he couldn't figure out what do next. Reading turned into a slow process of looking at pictures and picking up on a few key words, trying to figure out the subject of the magazine article. And Debbie began to fear leaving John alone.

Debbie is a warm, vibrant person who has a lot of friends, but in the first months after John came home from the hospital, she had a hard time leaving the house. She hesitated to go to the grocery store or to the pharmacy because she didn't want to encounter friends who would ask how John was. "I didn't want to go over the story one more time. It was so heavy and hard to talk about," she said. Debbie described the first two years after John's seizures as sorrowful. "John had to retire. We had no health and long-term care insurance. We were going to lose everything," she said.

John and Debbie had to let go of their retirement plans to volunteer for the World Health Organization in developing countries. The grandchildren that came after a second round of seizures "will never know the man John was," Debbie noted with sadness. Debbie had to come to terms with the fact that her partner and the man she had married was gone, and so was her independence. "I am always taking care of two people, John and myself," she says. "There is no one to take care of me."

But in time Debbie adjusted—and with incredible grace. I asked her what she had learned from the experience. Without hesitation and with a broad smile, she said, "I learned I could do anything!" Debbie had struggled through all the medical decisions and paperwork that resulted from her husband's seizures. She sold her husband's dentistry practice. She sold a house and moved. She remodeled and rearranged the house as his physical condition declined. "I didn't ask to learn how strong I am," she told me. "But I learned."

As Debbie and I sat outside at a small table at the coffee shop, we were interrupted several times. Each time a friend would walk by, see Debbie, and stop for a hug and a minute of conversation. Debbie had moved herself and John to an area of town where she could walk to do her shopping, sit by the lake, and see her friends. Debbie had gathered friends around her—friends whom she had known for thirty years and new friends. Debbie talked about how she was not afraid to ask a friend for help if that person knew something that she needed to know or could do something for her.

Debbie had surrendered to her situation by creating a life that was simple and that allowed her to be comfortable and whole. "The pain does not go away. I don't have the man I married, and my heart is forever broken. But I can live with that," she said as we parted. And before I left, I got a hug.

REFLECTION
You Can't Visit Me Where I Live

I was perplexed after I left Roberta's house. Roberta had just finished her caregiver journey after taking care of Sam for fifteen years. Sam had suffered from Parkinson's and dementia. At the beginning of our conversation, Roberta made it clear that a big piece of being a caregiver was isolation and feelings of loneliness. That I understood.

But what puzzled me were comments that she made later in our conversation. Now that Sam was gone, Roberta smiled when she described the joy she experienced when spending the evening alone doing what she wanted. Roberta talked about the pleasure she felt when she got up in the morning and went to get a cup of coffee and read the paper at the local coffee shop—alone.

Wasn't she alone most of the time when she was a caregiver? Why was "alone" such a different experience when she wasn't a caregiver? It took me several months to understand.

Other caregivers have told me stories of their feelings of loneliness and isolation. One caregiver became sad when one of her closest friends said, "I know how you feel. My father just died, and it was tough to be his caregiver." Caregiving for this friend involved flying in to visit her father once a month for the weekend. The caregiver sitting in front of me said, "My friend has no idea what it is like to take care of someone who is sick and dependent day after day, all day. I know my friend is trying to be supportive—but she does not understand my life right now."

Another caregiver remarked how hard it was to get together with a friend whom she had known all her life. "All she can talk about is the latest vacation she and her husband have taken and how great retirement is going to be for the two of them. My friend doesn't understand that all of that has been taken away from me. I am looking at years of being a twenty-four-hour nurse to my husband."

One caregiver cringes when asked how her husband is. "What am I supposed to say? Things are not good—and they are going to get worse. But that's not what people want to hear when they ask the question. So I just say fine and leave it at that."

If you're a caregiver, even your closest friends don't know what your life is like, because they don't follow you home. Home is where food has permanently stained the front of your spouse's shirt because he still is trying to feed himself. Home is where your spouse needs help shaving and putting on socks and shoes every morning. Home is where you are nurse, taxi driver, housekeeper, social director—manager of everything. Home is where you are experiencing the loss of your partner bit by bit, day by day.

After Roberta was done with her role of caregiver, being alone meant freedom. Being alone meant she could connect again with others about what excited her and her plans for the future. Being alone meant she could live her life and pursue her passions.

Alone became solitude, which Roberta enjoyed.

IV.

ACCEPTING
THE NEW NORMAL

MY STORY

It's All in How You Look at It

They say that it is all a matter of perspective. Everything is relative. In my case, that's very true.

At one point, my husband started to lose his short-term memory and ability to think things through. This was after losing many of his physical capabilities and his ability to talk above a whisper. None of this seemed fair. What more could Parkinson's take away from him?

When one of the doctors said that there was a medication that might help my husband's memory, it seemed like he was getting something back, for once.

We knew that the medication would have some short-term side effects—aches, pains, muscle cramping, sleepiness, and dizziness. We read all the disclaimers that came with the prescription from the pharmacy. The first few days weren't great; the side affects appeared, but at least we were prepared for them. Toward the end of the week, my husband woke up, came downstairs, and looked like his old self . . . for a few hours.

But he went downhill fast from there. By the next morning, he could not get out of bed by himself. He couldn't walk down the hall to the bathroom. He was obviously in pain and very disoriented.

That day we made a trip to urgent care, where as anticipated, they said to stop taking the new prescription. It would take a few days for the medication to get out of his body and then things would go back to "normal." Things continued to get worse for two days. It was hard to see my husband in such pain and have no way of giving him relief.

We decided to search out the neurologist. The moment my husband walked in the door of the clinic, his regular nurse could see something was wrong and took action. She discovered that the battery pack to his deep-brain-stimulation device had been turned off. She restarted his battery, and he immediately felt better. Within a day or two, he was back to "normal." This time the battery was the reason for the problem. This time things could be "fixed."

"Normal" has taken on new meaning for me. A few years ago, I would not have thought taking extremely slow walks around the block with my husband and the dog was normal. I would not have thought that conversations with my husband where I have to patiently wait for him to get his voice strong enough to be heard was normal. I would not have thought that laughing when my husband made fun of his illness was normal. I would not have thought that having Parkinson's was normal.

But that is my "new normal." And at the end of that week, I was thankful to have gotten back to that new normal. I also realized that the new normal wasn't all that bad. Slow walks let you notice the wind in the trees and the sun on your face. Patiently listening helps you really hear because each precious word is the product of hard work. We have learned that there is humor and joy in life when you stop trying to control life and accept things the way they are. My new normal is a gift I appreciate.

Love Him Up

Rose was forced to watch a robbery. Like a thief, the dementia, which so often comes with Parkinson's, robbed her husband of all his God-given abilities, bit by bit.

First, it took away his ability to remember where he had put things. Then it stole his ability to plan. (When he wanted to get from point A to point D, he could no longer figure out what or where points B and C needed to be.) Then he began to ask the same questions he had asked half an hour earlier. For him, getting through the day was like walking through fog that did not lift. Rose's competent executive husband no longer existed. Dementia was stealing him away.

At first dementia caused frustration, in both Rose and her husband. Rose's husband was frustrated because he knew he had been able to think things through before. Why couldn't he do that now? How come he couldn't do what he had been able to do . . . what he *should be able* to do? Rose was frustrated that all these changes demanded more and more of her. Their frustration turned into anger every time either of them tried to do something.

Then Rose discovered a different way to handle the dementia. She found that in the middle of the frustration, if she could "love him up," as she put it, his fear and frustration would melt away. When she showed her husband love, physical and emotional, he would relax and let her take care of him. The more she loved him up, the easier it was to work through things. They both could move through the situation more gracefully.

Rose's partner was becoming more and more childlike. When that was honored and celebrated through love, her husband reacted just like a good child. When children feel loved and secure, they are a true joy to be around.

The Resolute Advocate

Ann has been traveling the treacherous path of caregiving for years now—first, with her mother, and now her dad. When I talked to her, she made it clear that she had no training, skill, or talent in medicine or any desire to be nurse. She felt unequipped to deal with pain or the bodily processes of a sick parent. But what she was equipped to handle were the medical institutions. She became an advocate bridging the communication gaps between doctors, nurses, insurers, social workers, and administrators on behalf of her mother and then her dad.

Being an advocate for each of her parents was a choice, but a costly choice, for Ann. Over three years, Ann's mother had knee surgery, breast cancer, a stroke, and a fatal fall. The family took shifts for a month at the hospital to be with her mother every day. A family member assisted with daily rehab at the nursing home for six months, and a different family member came each night to help with bedtime routines and medications.

When I asked Ann why she felt she or a family member needed to be there all the time with her mother, Ann replied, "We saw all the mistakes they made. They were understaffed, and although they tried hard, there were too few staff for patients who had great needs. We couldn't sit by and see our mom treated like that." On the day that Ann's mother died, Ann's company restructured, and she lost her job.

A few years later, Ann's father was diagnosed with Parkinson's. At one point, there were nineteen doctor's appointments in nineteen days. It was Ann who talked to the doctors and helped her father sort out his treatment choices. At that time, Ann had a complex job that required long hours, a job that she had worked hard to get. But the mounting need to be both at the job and at the doctor's appointments eventually required a choice. She resigned from a job that she had pursued a master's degree to obtain.

Ann was clear that she wasn't a victim. "I made hard choices at every juncture. I didn't know what I was getting into, but I had to live with myself, so I made those choices. It was never obvious I would go for an extended time without an income. Who knew I was resigning a job just as the country slid into recession? It never occurred to me I would end up here. But I am proud of myself and proud my choices."

One of Ann's friends made the comment to Ann that she was "so lucky" to have been able to be with her mother during those final years. "I am not lucky. I paid for it dearly," said Ann. Ann was angry and hurt that her friend did not understand that caregiving for a person with a chronic disease like Parkinson's is a choice that comes with an unknown price tag, paid over an unknown amount of time. Ann and I wondered how many caregivers just leave because they can't or don't want to pay that price.

I asked Ann if she had any advice for those who were going to travel down a similar path. "Anyone who says they have your answer is full of shit," she said. "Any advice I could give would not fit someone else's situation. I have huge of empathy for those who have to navigate this road."

"Okay," I said. "Then how do you take care of yourself in the middle of all the chaos? How do you keep from sacrificing yourself to take care of your loved one?"

Ann answered, "Self-protection is part of what you learn as you go along. Figure out what is really important to you and live those things even if it has to be in small pieces. Try to develop scenarios—what if this happens, how can I best cushion myself against that? Ask your friends for specific help. If you need to work, maybe it is possible to work part time or find a job that has the flexibility to let you come and go as needed. But know yourself, learn about your own needs and don't let others tell you that you are wrong for being who you are. Caregiving is a complicated deal. The burden of care delivery has to be divided in a way that prevents cannibalizing the caregiver. The sick person has to acknowledge that the care partner has needs, too."

When the Student Is Ready, the Teacher Will Appear

Kathleen and I were meant to meet. We had gone to the same college just a few years apart. I had worked at two companies where her husband had worked. She and I had several professional colleagues in common. We even lived in the same neighborhood, a few blocks apart. Our husbands had been diagnosed with Parkinson's about the same time, and now we had Parkinson's in common.

Another thing that we had in common is lifelong training in taking care of everyone and everything—except ourselves. Kathleen had grown up with alcoholism in her family, so enabling was second nature to her. She had gone to school in social work and that had been her first profession. She also wanted to be accepted by her stepchildren, and when they realized this, they took advantage of it. "I had been trained to be responsible for everything, every wounded bird," she told me.

I asked Kathleen how Parkinson's had changed her life. Kathleen said, "Parkinson's taught me that I have to learn how to take care of myself. Giving up my life to take care of my husband is not going to take away my husband's Parkinson's. My husband's Parkinson's can't be the center of my life. I don't have a choice of whether my husband has Parkinson's, but I do have a choice about how I want to react to it and how I want to live my life."

This meant that Kathleen was making choices. She was willing to give up the idea of being self-employed and find a job in a company—for the healthcare benefits. But she was not willing to quit her job and become a full-time caregiver. She was willing to adapt their house to her husband's physical needs or move to a single floor home. But she was not willing to move to rural Georgia, where she knew no one, to be close to his relatives. She was willing to visit his kids on occasion but did not join him on every family event.

Kathleen was aware that she lived in two worlds at the same time. One world included her husband and the things that were bringing them closer together. The other world was one she was building for herself. This "single" life was built on choices of what she wanted for herself, now and in the future.

Kathleen summed it up by saying, "Parkinson's is here to teach me a life lesson. This life is all I have, and I don't want to spend it being a victim. I need to make choices that are good for me, not just for everyone else. If I don't learn this lesson now, I will have to learn it later." Then she quoted a Buddhist saying: "When the student is ready, the teacher appears. Parkinson's has brought me to this place to learn this lesson."

When I smiled and told her how much I admired her, she smiled back, "I have to learn this lesson every day."

Respect

Birgitta looks nothing like Aretha Franklin, but she understands the same thing that Aretha does. Everyone needs respect.

Birgitta came prepared to our meeting about caregiving. She had handouts for me. One was about the meanings behind care giving. Birgitta was very clear that the motives for caring for another person are important. Caregiving can be motivated by fear, fear of how others see us, the fear of feeling guilty, or the fear of not giving enough. Caregiving can be motivated by the need for approval, affirmation, and attention. Given these motivations, caregiving becomes selfish and serves our hidden agendas. These motivations leave little room for true love or respect—for the caregiver or the ill person. They belittle both people.

Birgitta's other handout was about the important difference between being responsible *for* another person and being responsible *to* them. Being responsible for another person put one in the position of fixing things, protecting, and rescuing. It puts the caregiver in a superior and controlling position. And with all the energy going out, the caregiver becomes exhausted, fearful, and liable for everything. When the caregiver shifts to an attitude of responsibility to another person, it opens up the relationship to a partnership where both people contribute what they can. The energy flows back and forth. Both people are valued and respected.

Birgitta lives by these values. Her husband is disabled and confined to a wheelchair by severe back problems. He also has Parkinson's. During a period of 113 days in which her husband had nine surgeries on his back, Birgitta found herself in a situation where she had to demand respect for her husband. There were doctors who wanted to shrug off the increasing decline in her husband's condition as the normal course of healing. The doctors were not willing to look at evidence that indicated that something was seriously wrong. Birgitta had to demand a second opinion that confirmed that her husband was getting worse and needed additional surgery to live.

Birgitta came to a point when her husband's life hung in the balance. Should he have risky surgery that could kill him or should he be left to deteriorate? In this situation, Birgitta chose a path of being responsible to her husband. It was not her decision alone. It was a decision that both of them made together.

On a daily basis, there are also many other decisions to make. When her husband doesn't want to do something, such as taking his medications, Birgitta points out that he has a choice. He can take his pills, or he can get worse and move to a care center or the VA hospital. But the decision is his.

Birgitta pointed out the difference between handicap-accessible and handicap-friendly. "A lot of places are handicap accessible. But theses places are not designed by people who know what it is like to push a wheelchair on certain types of carpet or up a small incline. Sometimes a handicapped person does not want to sit up front in a meeting room or other facility. They want to be in the back so it is not so far to get in and out. But most handicapped spots are right up front." Birgitta was pointing out that handicapped people are often not given the same choices as everyone else. They are not given that basic respect.

"Another example is the cart-return area at shopping centers. There is no cart-return area next to the handicapped-parking spot. I have often gone to a store to find a cart blocking the handicapped-parking space. I couldn't figure out why this happened so often. Then I realized that by the time they get back to the car with the cart and unload it. The additional distance they need to travel to put away the cart is too much."

Birgitta respects herself. When she was diagnosed with posttraumatic stress disorder (PTSD), she knew she needed professional help and she got it. She has people to come in to help her care for her husband during the day. She asks her children to step up and help her at regular times during the month. "I used to be a mom who did it all. I can't do that anymore, and it is good for the kids to see that," she said. Birgitta protects one hour at the beginning of the day for her prayer and meditation. (Her husband knows better than to interrupt her during this time!)

Birgitta has respect for herself and her husband. She understands the difference between being responsible TO someone and not FOR someone. Birgitta and her husband are still partners in life regardless of his illness or handicap.

REFLECTION

You Can't Answer Anyone Else's Heart Issues

If you are anything like me, you are all too willing to take on the burdens of others. I want to fix things for people. I want to make things "all better." That is why I would never be a good therapist or a good chaplain. Let me explain.

By chance one day I watched a DVD featuring an interview with a chaplain for terminally and chronically ill people. It set me to wondering: How does this person express daily love and caring for these ill people, yet manage not to be consumed by the pain? How does she bear the loss and grief she experiences day after day? How does she minister without depleting or sacrificing herself? So I went in search of some answers. I went in search of Sister Marian.

Sister Marian's role model for caregiving is Jesus. Invoking him isn't a simple matter of obligation for Sister Marian. She has given a lot of thought and study to how he actually operated when he helped people. And what she had concluded surprised me. Sister Marian cited example after example of how Jesus took care of *himself* and asked for help:

- The day Jesus got on a boat and went to the middle of the lake to get away from the crowds.

- The time Jesus let a woman wash his feet with expensive oil.

- The time Jesus went to a wedding as a guest, simply to celebrate.

- The time on Mount Tabor when Jesus surrounded himself with his closest friends.

- The time in the Garden of Gethsemane when he asked for the help of his disciples.

Jesus wasn't a compulsive caretaker. He didn't walk around all day searching for people to help and to cure. In fact, many times Jesus had to be asked to help before he finally stepped in.

Clearly, Jesus modeled not just great compassion, but clarity about his role—clarity about boundaries and self-care. In turn, Sister Marian talked about the line that has to be negotiated between the ill person and the caregiver. "The role of the caregiver is big—maybe bigger than that of the sick person. There needs to be a limit on how much can be asked of the caregiver. There is a point when the caregiver needs to enlist the help of professional caregivers and nursing facilities because others can do a better job. For every couple and family, that line is different. But it needs to be talked about."

Finally, Sister Marian said, "Don't make assumptions about people. Everyone is a different book and story. When confronted with a terminal or chronic illness, some people become focused on the purpose and goals for the remainder of their life. Certain things become important to them and other things fall away. Other people 'go for the gold.' They are determined to beat the odds that the medical community has given them. Other people are accepting of their fate. Their priority is how to live well, not how to be sick.

"Whatever the reaction, everyone has to pay attention to their own heart when they come to that point in life. It is a time that they have to decide for themselves what is important, what has been left unfinished, and how to spend the remaining time. All you can do is give permission to a person to talk and then listen to them. All you can do is ask questions and empower people to answer their own heart issues. All you can do is bear witness and journey with them. You can't answer anyone else's heart issues."

For the ill person and the caregiver, the new normal is different. Some of it is a given, nonnegotiable. Some it we can choose or mold. Each of us needs to work that out for ourselves . . . and with the one for whom we are caring. The important thing is that we pay attention to our heart and let it lead us forward.

V.

RENEWED

PLACES TO REFUEL

MY STORY

Seal Skin Soul Skin

There is a folk story that has been told in the Nordic, Irish, and Northwest American Indian traditions. It's the story of the selkies.

The selkies are sea creatures that can come up on land, take off their skins, and dance in the moonlight. One night a number of selkies came on shore and were dancing. A lonely fisherman saw them from his boat, landed it, and watched them from behind a bush. They were lovely. The fisherman saw their skins lying on the shore, and he hid one of them. When the selkies realized they were being watched, they scattered, grabbed their skins, and returned to the sea—except one, who could not find her skin. The fisherman had stolen it.

The fisherman was taken by the lone selkie's beauty and came up to her. "You can have your skin back after you marry me, have my children, and stay with me for seven years," he said. Having no choice, the selkie went with the fisherman, became his wife, and gave him a child.

After seven years the selkie went to her husband and asked for her skin back. The fisherman, who didn't want her to leave, reneged on his promise. He would not give her skin back and would not tell her where he had hidden it. When she realized she could not go home, she began to whither and die.

One day the selkie's child was walking around the cliff by the sea and spotted a wooden chest. In the chest was something strange—it looked like the skin of a sea creature. He quickly took it to his mother to find out what it was. Of course, it was her skin.

The selkie put her skin on, kissed her child good-bye, and returned to the sea to be the creature she was born to be. In the years that follow, she comes back to visit her child, and they have wonderful conversations on the shore.

This story is about renewal. If you don't have access to a place where you can go to renew yourself, to really *be* yourself, you will begin to whither and die. It doesn't mean that you have to give up the daily responsibilities that make up your life. It doesn't mean you need to run away from the energy-consuming things that challenge you. It doesn't mean that you will lose strength to fight life's battles. Quite the opposite: You need a place and time that leaves you renewed and gives you a sense of calm in order to build the strength to live and function in the world.

Probably by instinct, I found a means of renewal: artistic expression. One day I woke up and knew I wanted to weave. I bought a loom and began; my experiences with weaving on a floor loom making scarves and table runners took me to tapestry weaving. Tapestry weaving took me to design and full-fledged artistic expression.

Weaving creates a special place of peace for me, a place I go for an hour or two at a time. There the realities of the world and all of my responsibilities can recede into the background for a while. I find calm and vision that I did not know existed in me . . . or could come through me.

Everyone needs to have a selkie skin—call it a soul skin instead of a seal skin—that takes them to a place of reality and renewal.

Ask, Accept and Enjoy

I walked into the restaurant and immediately recognized Julie from church. She is a petite, classy-looking woman who seemed a bit weary that day. Julie's husband, Rob, has Parkinson's. Julie had just finished coping with her husband's surgery. The surgery had been hard on Rob, and the medical community's paperwork and regulations had been overwhelming for Julie. It seemed to me that Julie's daily life was entirely made up of trips to one doctor or another, time spent in one waiting room or another, and figuring out how to cope with her husband's reaction to the latest medical procedure he'd undergone. Despite her weariness, Julie's eyes were alive and kind. I could sense an inner strength, and I wanted to find out about it.

Julie was "blessed"—and I say that with great deal of sarcasm. This was her second caregiving assignment. First, she had taken care of her husband's mother, who had Parkinson's. Now, she was taking care of her husband, who had the same disease. (She has also seen one of Rob's siblings experience Parkinson's.)

I asked Julie what the hardest part of Rob's illness was for her. She began to talk about the losses she was experiencing. Last New Year's Eve she learned that a group of couples she and Rob had known for many years had gotten together to celebrate. "They just assumed that we wouldn't come. They didn't even bother to ask," she said with sadness. "We don't get included anymore because Rob is disabled. I am losing my relationship with these friends because of Rob's illness.

"I have also lost the freedom to do things spontaneously. We used to go out to eat or to the movies when we felt like it. We went on vacation every winter to Florida. Now we don't go on vacation anymore. I have to plan everything around medical appointments, medication schedules, and what Rob can eat. It is like having a baby again."

Finally, Julie talked about the loss of her partner. "When the furnace broke last December, I had to figure out what to do and make all the decisions. Before, I would discuss these things with Rob." Now everything was her responsibility to manage and get done.

And what if Julie passed away before Rob? Julie went on to describe all the financial planning she had done in case something happened to her. She created an emergency fund that her brother could use to take care of Rob. She established an estate, put together wills, and power of attorney documents. All this she thought out and decided—alone.

I asked Julie if she had any advice for others, like me, who were facing the same situation. She quickly responded, "Ask for help and take it!"

Julie found daily support in her morning phone call with her sister, who had also recently suffered a significant family loss. "We talk and help each other think things through. We know what each other is dealing with."

Julie is also very lucky. Her daughter and son have stepped up and are there for her. Her daughter comes every Wednesday to spend the night, take the night shift with her father, and give Julie some time on Thursday to get out of the house. All the kids, in-laws, and grandkids help out by taking care of household chores and repairs. They take Rob to appointments and help run errands from time to time. Julie is not alone.

But Julie has learned to ask for help beyond her engaged family network. "Doctors have resources or know where to get assistance," she points out. Through one of Rob's doctors, Julie has found an advocate who procured additional in-home help for Julie. This gives her a modicum of free time.

"The in-home provider told me that a lot of caregivers don't know what to do with these hours of freedom," said Julie. "I know how *I'm* going to use that time! I'm going to have my hair done and have lunch with some friends."

After Julie wakes Rob in the morning, he always asks, "Have you taken your deep breath yet?" That's how Julie's day starts. She takes a deep breath, asks for help from those around her, and uses that help to take care of Rob *and* herself.

Find Your Rock in the Sun

A sanctuary is a place of refuge. It is a place apart where it is safe and you can separate yourself from the things that hang heavy on you. It is a place to hide and renew yourself—even if it is only for a short time. That is what Ann has created at the Briar Patch Resort.

As you descend the hill into Briar Patch, you are enveloped by nature. The sounds of cars and airplanes are replaced by the rustle of the wind in the trees and the rush of running water in the creek. A sculpture of Saint Francis of Assisi greets you at the door of the lodge. Polly greets you at the reception desk. If you have been to Briar Patch before, you are greeted like a good friend who has been away too long.

Each cottage at Briar Patch is unique and has been created by Ann. Navajo rugs hang on the walls and handcrafted crosses hang above the beds. The bed covers are handmade by women from around the world. Recesses in the wall are altars consecrated to artwork from the far-off lands that Ann has visited. Each cottage has a patio, a fireplace, and a vase of fresh flowers. There are no phones or televisions. There is no Wi-Fi.

Your reason for being there is to be there. You can sit by the creek. You can find trails to hike, and you can explore the canyon. You can watch the birds and listen to their songs. You can visit a family of sheep. If you are ambitious, there are books to borrow and read. If you are wise, you will have a massage in the outdoor (and private) gazebo overlooking the creek.

Ann has created a sanctuary for others here.

Ann's husband, Richard, was diagnosed with Parkinson's in his early fifties. This past year he died in his sixty-eighth year. All those years Ann was the creative spirit of Briar Patch . . . and Richard's caregiver.

Ann learned to be independent during those years. She figured out how to make a living in a way that supported her family and that used her creative talents. Her family would step in at least once a year so that she could travel and bring back treasures of the heart and hand from distant places. She created a family at Briar Patch and now watches over the welfare of the people who work there.

But Ann also learned how to eat dinner by herself on nights that Richard went to bed at five in the afternoon. At times, it was hard to think of Richard as a husband and partner—so much of her time was consumed with taking care of him. There was sadness in her eyes when she talked about never being invited to another couple's house for dinner—and how few people treated her husband as a friend rather than someone with a debilitating disease.

Being newer to caregiving than Ann, I asked, "How did you take care of yourself during all those years?" All I could think of was how exhausted I was—and I was just beginning the journey. Ann answered by telling me about the hiking she did in the canyon and by the creek. One day she found a large rock by the creek on which she could sit to soak up the sun. She would go back to that rock from time to time. That was *her* sanctuary. Then with a thoughtful look in her eye, Ann said, "Everyone needs a place to go like that, even if the visit is only in his or her mind."

As I left Briar Patch, Ann gave me one last hug and said, "Find your rock in the sun . . . and get a massage from time to time." During that weekend, Ann helped me understand the importance a finding a sanctuary where I can go to renew myself. I will be going back to Briar Patch from time to time—sometimes physically, sometimes only in my memory.

The Ring

Chris and her husband were taking their dream vacation, before her husband (who had Parkinson's) was unable to travel. The responsibilities of home, work, doctors, and kids started to melt away the moment their cruise ship left the dock. Soon they would be in a time zone eight hours from home. Soon their cell phones and their e-mail would no longer work.

Life aboard the ship was a world unto itself. You could wake up when you wanted. You could take a nap or go to bed when you felt like it. There was always someone around to feed you and entertain you . . . or you could be alone. Chris found this life strange and at times disconcerting. She was so used to being in charge of a demanding schedule and reacting to the needs of others. Flipping the switch was a challenge, but one she wanted to try.

One evening toward the end of the cruise, she and her husband dressed up for the evening's five-course dinner and drinks in the bar. Her little black dress came out of the closet for the second time since she had bought it. The cashmere shawl, which she had bought on the trip, looked perfect with the dress. That night Chris spent a few more minutes on her hair and makeup.

After the two-hour dinner, Chris and her husband moved to the piano bar to listen for a while before they retired to their cabin. Next to the piano bar area was the cruise ship boutique, which was having a sale on costume jewelry. Chris wandered over to the sale table.

"I saw a faux-diamond ring a little larger than the one I have always fanaticized about having. I have no use for a ring like that, especially one so big. I have more jewelry than I can wear at one time. Sure, it was only forty dollars worth of glass, but I still said no to it. I didn't need it."

But after two glasses of wine, and with her husband's encouragement, Chris went back and bought the ring. For the rest of the evening, Chris had fun flashing her ring around and feeling attractive in her little black dress.

The next morning and through out the day, Chris's thoughts kept going back to the ring she had bought the night before. Why did she buy it? She wouldn't wear it that often. It was way too gaudy too wear to work, and she rarely went places where she had to dress up. Maybe the boutique would take it back.

After spending way too much time thinking about her whimsical purchase, it hit her. "I needed to keep the ring—and to wear it. I wanted the ring regardless of whether I needed it or deserved it. I am always asking my husband, my kids, and my workplace what they need from me. Then I figure out how to make it happen. But I never ask the question: What do I want? What do I need?

"I started to cry when I realized how empty and exhausted this left me. So I am going to keep the ring to remind me to ask the question, What do I want? once in a while. I am going to wear the ring to remind myself that I deserve forty dollars worth of bling because it makes me smile and feel extravagant, if even for a few minutes."

Knots

LuAnn had been dealing with Parkinson's for ten years, ever since Jeff, her husband, had been diagnosed with the disease.

During the first few years after Jeff's diagnosis, things were okay. There was always the fear of what the future was sure to bring, but since Parkinson's had not so far kept either LuAnn or Jeff from doing the things that they wanted to do, LuAnn could push the fear to the back of her mind for another day.

Then there were the "middle" years. Parkinson's became a much more frequent visitor. Although Jeff could function fairly well, signs of the disease were showing up more and more often. It was becoming harder and harder for the couple to continue their normal life. Then came the day Jeff had to retire because he could no longer function at work.

Now LuAnn prepared for the "siege." Parkinson's was now a permanent and unwelcome part of the family.

"How are *you* doing?" I asked.

"I am doing better than I was," LuAnn answered. "My body has always been something I have taken care of. But when times got busy these past few years and I had to come through, I told my body to suck it up and keep going. Finally, my body said, 'No more.'"

"What do you mean?" I asked. "You look so healthy and full of energy."

"My body just said, 'Stop'. I started to feel a tiredness that would not go away. My daily runs became impossible; I could hardly get around the block. When I ignored that as best I could, my body started screaming. I had always carried tension in my shoulders. Now I couldn't turn my head without pain and my jaw started to hurt."

"So what did you do?"

"At first I did nothing. It was my husband who was sick, not me. And even if I did admit that things were not quite right, my husband was still sicker than I was, wasn't he? My job was to pick up the slack and keep going."

LuAnn found the medical community was not helpful when it came to her health issues. When she suffered from fatigue, her doctors tested her for West Nile virus, hormone imbalances, parasites, and anything else they could think of. LuAnn finally got tired of paying them to take her blood for tests.

When she had numbness in her leg, the doctors tested her for a stroke and a pinched nerve. When these tests turned out negative, they shrugged their shoulders and sent her on her way. The dentist told her the pain in her jaw came from grinding her teeth at night and gave her a mouth guard. The pain stopped getting worse . . . but it didn't get better.

Out of desperation, LuAnn finally took her friend's advice and went to a massage therapist. After the first massage, LuAnn felt worse. Her muscles didn't like being told to relax, and they rebelled. After a few more massages, LuAnn could identify the knots in her body that had built up over the years. Slowly the pain subsided.

"As the knots in my muscles started to untie, the knots in my life started to loosen," said LuAnn. "I started to think that maybe all the to-dos I had to accomplish each day were not equally important. I started to realize that bracing myself for the horrible future that I envisioned wasn't going to help me deal with it. It was going to be what it was going to be, and I could figure it out as it came. I started to ask myself what things brought me joy every day, to help balance out the challenges and losses."

LuAnn's emotional knots also loosened up. As LuAnn sat in front of me, I had the image of someone floating in the ocean. The waves were coming onto the shore. But instead of trying to swim against the waves and wearing herself out, LuAnn was floating on top of them. She could still feel their power and motion, but she was no longer fighting them.

REFLECTION

Faith—To Believe or Not to Believe; That Is the Question

As we progress on our journeys as caregivers, there are many people who take solace in their faith and in daily prayer. Does this faith practice make it easier to carry the burdens of care giving? No matter what tradition you come from, faith means you believe in something that you cannot see, touch, or hold in your hand. What about my faith? After pondering that question, this is what I came up with.

I believe that there is a God, a creative force for good. It is amazing to me that this God created me. I celebrate the fact that God is giving me another day to live, another creative thought, another insight, and another flower to enjoy. It is amazing to me that just when things are the darkest and I am running on empty, this God finds me and gives me what I need to carry on.

I believe in prayer. Not just the kind that you do when you kneel, put your hands together, and close your eyes. Prayer is when you let your soul talk to God and share genuine, honest feelings—fear, anger, joy, laughter. Prayer is living life. Prayer is thanking the universe for what you have, asking for what you need, and blessing what you get.

I believe that I will get what I need—and more. It may not be what I ask for or what I think I should get. (If I did get everything I wanted, I would end up a spoiled child who thinks the world is there to serve her.) God has wisdom beyond my small understanding of the universe and knows why I am here.

I believe that God created me for a purpose, however simple or grand that purpose may be. My job is to stay silent enough to hear what that purpose is and get on with it.

So what does all this mean for my life as a caregiver?

It means that life is bigger than my husband's disease. I may not understand how or why this is true, but it is. And I cannot let this disease rob my husband or me of our souls.

It means I will get the wherewithal to get up in the morning and get through the day—I hope, with a little grace and humor. It means I have to recognize the gifts I have received and will receive—gifts that I may not have asked for and may not deserve. Then I need to graciously accept and celebrate those gifts.

As my days of caregiving get more challenging, I pray to God to give me some faith. With that, I know I can get through each day, and sometimes even celebrate the day, one day at a time.

So what do you believe in?

VI.

UNEXPECTED GIFTS

THERE IS A PONY
IN THERE

MY STORY

A Sad Story and a Bad Joke

I called Caroline on the phone. It was her husband's birthday that day. He had died the previous January at the age of seventy-seven after battling Parkinson's disease for ten years. Caroline and Frank had been married fifty-seven years.

As I listened to Caroline talk, I experienced a growing tightness in my stomach. My first thought was that I was uncomfortable hearing what was in store for me. And that was true. I didn't like hearing about this athletic, active man losing his ability to do the things he loved, like running. I didn't like hearing about the fact that it took Caroline two hours in the morning to bathe and feed her husband. I didn't like hearing that caregiving has taken over their marriage and relationship.

But the other thing that Caroline said several times during our conversation was: "I kept asking Frank what he was thinking."

With the luxury of observation from a distance, my belief was that Frank suffered from depression that often times comes with Parkinson's. After the diagnosis and after his capabilities began to diminish, Frank became distant from his family and friends. He did not want to do anything with them. He didn't communicate well with his kids when they tried to engage him. He would go away by himself for hours. When friends came over, Frank wouldn't come out of the kitchen and join the party. And Frank would never answer Caroline's question: "What are you thinking?"

Then I realized that Caroline had lost Frank well before he died. That realization was what was making me feel so uneasy and sad. I was lonely for Caroline and all the caregivers who soldier on in solitude.

After that call, I walked into the TV room and began thinking about what we were going to have for dinner. My husband was sitting on the couch after his nap. He looked at me with a crooked grin on his face and said, "I guess I lost my chance to woo you with romance before the kids come home."

I looked at him and smiled. His face had the wonderful look of a kid who had just told an off-color joke and had gotten away with it because the joke was so good.

My husband has Parkinson's, and we deal with all the terrible things that it is doing to both our lives. But in that moment, my husband had just told me that he still wanted to be with me. He had just shown me the grace by which he is living with an awful disease. He reminded me that I still had the essence of my husband with me in these moments and that I should not waste them. I felt grateful that I had realized the gift I have, a husband who truly loves me. And then I thanked God I still had my husband, Parkinson's and all.

I Wouldn't Have Missed It for the World

Deborah met me at her front door. She looked surprised to see me, and I was surprised at her surprise. I had made an appointment with her a week and a half earlier, and then I had called her on my way to her office. "I'm sorry, I can't do it today. My friend Evelyn just died," Deborah explained. After a few more words of conversation, I ended up staying, and we finished our work together. But the real event of the afternoon was Deborah's story about Evelyn.

Deborah had chosen to accompany her friend on the journey of Parkinson's. Deborah was not family, just a friend of many years. She had participated in Evelyn's venturesome and generous life over the decades. Deborah had celebrated the trips that Evelyn had taken to far-off lands. Deborah was there to remember Evelyn's birthdays and to celebrate the holidays with her. Deborah was the one who met Evelyn's later-in-life "boyfriend" and gave the relationship her "seal of approval."

In return, Evelyn had been a second mother to Deborah, watching the progress of her studies at school; supporting her research project overseas, both financially and emotionally. Deborah had gotten married in Evelyn's backyard.

When Evelyn's Parkinson's started to take hold, Deborah was the one who took Evelyn to the doctor, shopped for groceries, and cleaned Evelyn's apartment. When Evelyn's Parkinson's and dementia moved in permanently, Deborah was the one who took over the management of her friend's life and made daily visits to the nursing home.

As I was trying to find a nice way of asking Deborah "Why did you take on all that? You weren't family," Deborah must have known what I was going to ask. Her face broke out into a bright smile in spite of overwhelming fatigue. "I wouldn't have missed it for the world!" she said.

Deborah then went on to tell a sweet story about Evelyn. Evelyn found love at an advanced age—seventy-five. She met him on a trip to California to see some relatives. According to Evelyn, he was handsome and wonderful. She fell in love the first time they met. Most of their relationship was long-distance. He would not move to Minnesota, and she couldn't move to California. But their almost daily conversations on the phone brought them very close.

They were both well traveled and loved to talk about not only all the places they had visited but all the places they wanted to see together. Both of them were well read and up on current events. So the conversation was never dull, especially since Evelyn was a Democrat and her boyfriend was a Republican.

Toward the end of Evelyn's battle with Parkinson's, Deborah made the calls to Evelyn's boyfriend so that he and Evelyn could talk. At the very end, when Evelyn couldn't remember much of anything, Evelyn would hear her boyfriend's voice on the phone and her shoulders would relax; a calm would come over her. When Evelyn could no longer speak words, she whispered and cooed sounds of love over the phone to him. During those conversations, Deborah would sit close, feeling the glow of unconditional love between Evelyn and her boyfriend . . . and between Evelyn and Deborah.

At the end of a person's life, if you are lucky, you stand as a witness to that person's being on earth. If you're really lucky, you stand as a witness to the essence of their being. The greatest gift is to witness a person whose essence is generosity, love, and tenderness. Deborah was a lucky person.

I Like the Way He Looks at Me

Heather came into the Parkinson's Caregivers Support Group a little late. Getting out of the house with Dan, her husband, had taken a bit longer than "normal." And, of course, when she tried to hurry in order to be on time, it took even longer.

We all knew about Dan. He was losing the "executive" part of his mental capacity. This meant he was losing a big part of who he was—a bright, take-charge manager who kept things organized both at home and at work. Now figuring out the "next step" was a challenge for him.

Mother's Day had just passed. Heather had expected little in the way of gifts. Her kids didn't have a lot of money of their own. And Heather hadn't expected Dan to anticipate the day in time to do any shopping. "I assumed we would get together for a meal, one that I did not have to cook, and we would have a good time together," Heather said.

The night before Mother's Day, Dan pulled out a mail-order catalog to show Heather the gifts he had picked out and ordered that very day. Clearly, his ability to make appropriate choices was disappearing. "He ordered four cocktail dresses, a floppy sun hat, and a scarf that didn't match anything of mine. I would never wear any of these things. We rarely get out of the house even to run errands anymore, let alone to socialize. We don't go to parties or vacation at beach resorts," Heather said.

"But there was a 'gift' in the choices Dan had made. All the items showed me his genuine generosity. Money was no concern when it came time to give me a gift. He had also chosen a sexy, low-cut black cocktail dress for me. When I put it on, Dan smiled and said, 'I like that one on you.' His smile was worth everything to me—and I liked the way he looked at me," Heather told the group.

Heather's real gift on that Mother's Day was the knowledge that her husband still saw her as a sexy, good-looking woman whom he loves dearly. The generosity of his gift showed Heather the essence of who he is, an essence that will not be taken away by his terrible disease.

The Gift of Closure

Elizabeth's relationship with her father was strained. While she was growing up, he had worked hard to provide for the family, to give Elizabeth and her siblings a comfortable life. They all grew up healthy and went on to college, but after they graduated Elizabeth's father decided he no longer wanted to participate in their lives in any way. Apparently, he had decided to give up the emotional side of fatherhood.

When Elizabeth's father was diagnosed with Parkinson's, it didn't seem to make much difference in her life; after all, she was an adult with her own family, living in a different city. Even as his health worsened, she kept her distance from her father's life just as he had kept his distance from hers. Her mother took on the role of caregiver.

But one day Elizabeth woke up and felt the urge to go sit at her father's bedside. She had no particular reason to go. There was no drastic turn of events that precipitated her action. But she felt compelled to go. "Was it God or was it my dad calling me? I don't know," she said.

Elizabeth sat at her father's bedside for two days. They didn't say much to one another, since he could no longer communicate with words. But on the second evening, Elizabeth blurted out, "I love you, Dad." He grunted back.

The next day Elizabeth's father died. When they carried his body out of the room, Elizabeth burst into tears that had been years in coming. She told me that at that moment she felt that she finally had closure. "We ended on good terms," she said. "I am so lucky to have been there before my dad died. It gave us a chance to heal some of the wounds and take care of unfinished business. I had been carrying around the heavy weight of isolation and resentment toward my father for years. We didn't even need words to make this happen. Ultimately, we just needed to forgive each other and express our love. We were able to part from each other with a sense of peace."

The Head of the AWOA

Pam was in her home office when her husband, Joe, walked in looking like he was on a mission. He plopped down in a chair and announced, "I got an important call this afternoon."

Pam stopped what she was doing. Joe had her attention. Then Pam's son wandered in, home from work.

"The head of the AWOA called," Joe reported. "He said he was going to lose his job if things didn't change."

"What job? What in the world is AWOA?" Pam asked.

"The Ass Wipers of America," said Joe. "This guy's responsibility is to shoot holes in toilet paper rolls and insert the cardboard tube in the toilet paper. He said that he is getting reports that no one in this family is using the hole in the roll. Whenever the toilet paper roll is empty in this house, people just take a new roll and put in on the counter. They leave the empty cardboard roll on the holder. If we don't start using the hole in the toilet paper roll, this guy is going to lose his job!"

Pam burst out laughing, and her son looked perplexed. The more confused her son looked, the harder she laughed. Eventually, Joe couldn't keep a straight face and broke out laughing, too.

"Parkinson's and its effects continue to rob me of the husband I once knew," Pam told me. "But in another way you could say it's distilling him down to his essence. And I am finding I cherish this essence. He is more affectionate and playful than I noticed in those busier days of juggling jobs and kids. Parkinson's is not a gift. But it can't take way the true spirit of a person. I celebrate the playful spirit that still lives in the man I married a long time ago."

Hindsight Is 20/20

Certain things are easier to see in hindsight. That's the perspective that Harriet brought to our caregiver group.

Harriet's husband had died a few years earlier after suffering for a decade with Parkinson's. Harriet was his caregiver almost to the end. She continued to come to our caregiver group to listen to our frustration, anger, and grief—and to testify to the fact that we current caregivers would be okay. It was her way of "paying it forward." Listening to her, we hoped that we would end up better than okay, like Harriet.

Harriet talked about some important things she had learned, especially in the final and hardest days. "I would not have survived if I hadn't let go of my desire to get things done and get them done perfectly," she told us. "While I was working and raising kids I had to be organized and efficient, and things worked out pretty well.

"But when Parkinson's took over my life, I had to learn that I didn't have control anymore. I could plan a day only to find myself doing something else. An unexpected trip to the emergency room could take over the whole day. My husband would come home without his glasses and I was back in the car retracing his steps to find them. My ability to get through my list of to-do's was totally dependent on how my husband was doing that day and how much help he needed.

"When I realized that having control in my life was impossible, I decided not to get upset when things didn't go as planned. I learned to 'go with the flow.' I learned that not everything is equally important. Getting the right two things done that day was good enough, and the rest of my list would wait for the next day.

"And forget perfection. If I cleaned up the house, my husband would pull out a box of things, empty it in the middle of the floor, and leave it there. I dressed my husband in clean clothes, and after one snack, most of his food was on his shirt front.

"Things just got done, and it was good enough. It was good enough that I washed clothes and that they stayed in a pile on the couch until I picked out my socks from the pile to wear them. It was okay that two out of the six light bulbs in the bathroom were out. My husband's medications got ordered and were sorted into the tray. But it was fine when I had to pay extra to get a prescription filled at the local pharmacy because I didn't notice that a medication was low and the mail order wouldn't come fast enough.

"I learned to move more slowly, on what you could call Parkinson's time. It would take my husband two or three times longer to do something than it took anyone else. And if you tried to rush things, it only took longer.

"If I took plenty of time to help my husband get dressed, things went more smoothly. If my husband 'froze' and couldn't move his feet to start walking, I discovered that taking the time to count 'one, two, three' to help him get going was better than watching him fall. If I had the patience to wait for my husband to collect the words he needed to talk to me, I was rewarded with an interesting thought or maybe a joke. When I took the time to walk—slowly—around the block with my husband, I noticed new things about my neighborhood that I had not seen in the twenty-five years I'd lived there. I guess you would call it 'being in the present' and focusing on what was in front of me.

"At first, when the responsibilities mounted and there were more and more things for me to do, I would obsess about the future. If I was having a hard time now, how would I survive when things got worse? (And they would get worse.) But I learned to take each day one at a time, and I always got through what I needed to get through that day. A friend would show up and help me do that one thing I needed an extra pair of hands for. Another caregiver would show me an easier way to do something, making my life just a little easier, too. When I needed to figure out how to do something, an expert would show up to help me.

"I'm not saying that the last couple of years weren't hard and exhausting. But with hindsight, I can see that I got some tools for life that I wouldn't have had otherwise. I learned that I didn't need to carry the extra burdens that I was carrying: 'never enough' and 'never good enough.' I learned I always got just enough. And I learned to be present with my husband while he was still with me. My life is different now that he is gone. But I have realized that those lessons apply to my 'new' life as well as my 'old' one."

REFLECTION
Vocation—Discovering a New Path

I identify with Moses. Before he was called by God, he was living the good life in the house of Pharaoh; before I found my vocation, my life was quite nice, too.

I had a great family—two close-to-perfect kids and a wonderful partner who wanted the best for me. I had a responsible job with all the things that make a responsible job fun—good assignments, titles, pay, promotions, visibility. Life was not just pretty good. It was great.

Then my life changed, just like Moses's did. It happened the day my husband was diagnosed with Parkinson's. I spent the next few years in denial, angry, and depressed. I kept trying to bargain with God and the medical community. I did not want the assignment of being a spouse to someone who had a chronic disease that was only going to get worse. I did not want to lose the rich life I had worked so hard to create. I did not want to lose my partner and my friend.

Like Moses, I kept trying to get out of it. Moses said, "Who am I to go to Pharaoh and bring the sons of Israel out of Egypt?" When that didn't get Moses off the hook, he tried a different ploy: "What if they do not believe me or listen to my words . . . ?" Then he protested: "I have never been a man of eloquence . . . I am a slow speaker and not able to speak well." Finally, Moses said, "If it pleases You, my Lord . . . send anyone else!"

Like Moses, I didn't feel up to the job that was thrust on me. I didn't feel equipped, physically or emotionally, to handle my husband's Parkinson's. Unlike many girls, I never wanted to be a nurse when I was growing up. I am not a patient, gentle person by nature, or someone who enjoys taking care of people.

But God didn't let Moses off the hook, and He didn't let me off the hook either.

Once I accepted the fact that this was my lot in life (and this did not come easily or quickly), God started to do some amazing things through me.

The first thing that happened was that I found refuge in tapestry weaving. At first it was my way of escaping. I would go into my weaving room after a long day, tired and cranky. I would come out of the room a calmer person after weaving awhile. Then I found a master weaver and artist who become my mentor and teacher. She helped me find my artistic voice. After a few years, I was able to exhibit and share my work with others. Creating has become a big part of my life; it renews me.

The other thing that I started to do is to collect stories from other caregivers. The caregiver's journey is hard and lonely. I thought that if I could share my stories and the stories of others, people in the midst of their journey would not have to feel as lonely, guilty, and hopeless as I did for so long.

In collecting these stories, I have met some incredible people, some of them true saints. These people are not perfect, not always cheerful and/or selfless. But they are all brave, compassionate, and loving. Their strength and wisdom are amazing as they deal with the challenges that life has given them. And each one of them is finding his or her way into and through the caregiver role with creativity and dignity. The gift they have given me and others is this book.

Who we are apart from our role as caregiver is important. Caregiving touches every part of our lives, but it does not have to consume or define us. We can find streams of energy and renewal running through our challenging lives. These streams truly enrich us and help us to come out the other end of the caregiving experience alive and whole.

VII.

EPILOGUE

THE BLESSING OF THE SAINTS

The group of caregivers was assembled for their monthly time together. Each had a story to share. All were living with the same burden—their spouse had Parkinson's disease. Usually the time was spent sharing frustrations, telling stories that were both heartbreaking and funny, and asking for advice. The beauty of the group was that no one had to explain why they felt the way they felt. Everyone just knew. But today was different. Three women had become widows in the past month.

Marge was the first one to speak. Her offering today was the understanding and wisdom gained by having to put her husband of fifty-some years in a care facility. She had promised her husband that she would never do that. But his limbs had become useless to him and his last fall at home had been the wake-up call. The dead weight of his body falling over took her with him, her head missing the corner of the kitchen counter by less than an inch.

Marge shared that once she had made the decision and moved her husband to the facility, she realized that it really was the best thing for everyone. Professionals took over his daily care and did a better job than she could have. In addition, her husband seemed to come out of his shell when surrounded by others during the day. His sense of humor came back. As he moved to the patio with a visitor, he would turn to the nurse at the desk and say, "Hold my calls," as if he were a CEO or a guest at a swanky resort. And the time that Marge and her husband had left was good time. She was his wife again, not his nurse. She was at peace with what she had to do. Marge wanted the same for us when we faced a similar situation.

She gave a blessing to the women in the room that day who were facing the same guilt-ridden decision, one they had never wanted to make. Marge said that things would be okay . . . and probably better.

Joan talked next. Her prayer for us was a peaceful death for our loved ones. She was still sorting out what happened to her husband not long before. He had been "fine" (at least in "new normal" Parkinson's terms). Then one night he did not wake up.

The last two years had not been peaceful for Joan's husband. They had been full of pain and frustration. But the words of comfort that she needed to hear came from the doctor: "Your husband died peacefully."

That's what Joan wished for all of our spouses as they, and we, followed her down the same path. Our partners' deaths were inevitable. But Joan prayed that our husbands would have a peaceful passing, and that this would give us the same peace she had found when the time came.

Mary was the last widow to talk. When she spoke up, it was in tears and confusion. She had lost her husband, upon whose energy she had relied for fifty-three years. She didn't know what to do next. She didn't know what she wanted. She wasn't quite sure who she was without her husband. This time the group blessed Mary.

A few people in the group had preceded Mary on this particular journey. One woman said, "After my husband died, everyone asked me what I was going to do now. No one asked me who I was going to *be* now. It takes time to answer that question."

That was Mary's next challenge—to redefine herself and her life. Others in the room were there to tell her they had done it, and that she could do it. The group prayed for Mary as she started her new journey. They blessed her as she took a deep breath and thought about how to start.

Many blessings were given that day. The group blessed those who had passed away by remembering the essence of their beings, the good times they had shared with their wives, and their bravery in facing Parkinson's.

Blessings were given by those who knew the road of those who were following. These blessings held the knowledge and wisdom that the followers were going to be battle-tested but would be stronger for their fight. Blessings of comfort and strength were given by those who "knew without being told."

Living with and giving care to a spouse with Parkinson's disease is a life-changing role. Parts of the journey are very hard. There is anger about losing a loved one bit by bit. There is anger about losing the life you had planned and worked for. There is fear about what is coming and fear that you won't be able to handle it. There is sadness about what you are losing—grief for the loss of your spouse and your life.

Other parts of the journey show you the unexpected gifts. You find that you are stronger than you ever imagined. You discover what is really important in your life, and you rejoice in the things that feed your soul. You may discover a richer role to play in life. You will see the essence of your loved one as Parkinson's takes his or her external abilities away.

I wish you blessings on your journey. Many have passed this way. They didn't choose to travel this road. But they are more compassionate and stronger because they made the trip. You will be as well.

VIII.

A GUIDE FOR FRIENDS
OF CAREGIVERS

I belong to an incredible group of women who are caregivers for their husbands. We meet once a month to talk about all the things friends and family cannot understand no matter how empathetic and caring they are.

At one of the meetings, I asked the group to tell me, and now you, the things that were not helpful to them on their long journey with Parkinson's—and what they really did need from their friends and family. Here are some of their comments and thoughts. We hope they are helpful to you as you try to support us.

Don't ask me how I am doing.

I don't want to think about how hard my life is, and is going to be. And, if I did acknowledge how bad things are, I know you probably don't want to hear about it. So I will just lie to you and say things are good.

It is better to ask me about how my day is going. I have learned to deal with each day as it comes. Some days are hard, and some days are good. But I can handle reflecting on today.

Don't ask me what you can do to help me.

I have learned that most of you really don't mean it because your lives are busy and full. Also, when you ask that question, you have now put the burden back on me to figure out what I need, to ask for the help and to manage it. It becomes easier to just do it myself.

If you truly want to help, suggest something you can do for me—something that takes an item off my plate of "to-dos." Then just do it. It can be simple things like bringing dinner every other Friday so that I don't have to cook. Tell me you will mow my lawn every week during the summer or shovel the snow.

(I have also been told by my friend, who really does want to help, to make a list of little things I need. So when she asks, I can suggest something without thinking and she does not have to guess what is helpful. There are friends who would feel good about helping if they knew what to do.)

Don't tell me to take care of myself or that I need to do more outside activities.

I know that. When you say that, it feels like one more thing to add to my to-do list and that is a long list already. It's all I can do to get through the day sometimes.

If you really mean it, ask me what I would do if I had a few hours to myself. Then show up and give me that time on a regular basis. It can be a luxury to shop for groceries at a leisurely pace and not have to figure out how to get someone to watch my husband so I can dash out. Ask me about things I do now that give me energy. Maybe I can find a few minutes to do a little more of what I am already doing to refuel myself.

Don't say "I know how hard it is to be a caregiver" if you are visiting your family member with a chronic disease once a week at the nursing facility.

Someone has already been hired to do the heavy labor. You have no idea how hard it can be if you don't have those resources or options—or you chose to take on caregiving full time. I know you want to empathize, but don't pretend you know what I am going through because you don't.

Acknowledge you don't know what it is to be a full-time caregiver. Ask me specific questions that you are truly interested in and want to know the answer like, "What is the hardest time of day for you? What is the most challenging thing you do?" Then be quiet and listen.

Don't spend all your time asking me how my husband is.

My life is consumed by Parkinson's as well. All of my time and resources are consumed by taking care of my husband. I don't want to talk about the new plateau we just arrived at that has brought new difficulties for him and defines our "new normal."

Acknowledge that Parkinson's has taken my life away as well, even though I do not have the disease. Then I know you do understand and care about me as well as my husband. Ask me how it has changed my life or what I miss from the pre-Parkinson's days. Then just listen.

Don't say "It must be hard."

It's not helpful. I have come to accept things and know they are what they are. They are not going to change. I also have no room in my life for pity or to feel sorry for myself.

Again, if you are genuinely interested, ask me what is the most challenging for me. Ask me what the hardest part of the day is for me. I can respond to specific questions. I will know you genuinely care and you are not giving me another platitude.

Don't say "You take such good care of him" or "You are so good to stand by him through these hard times."

I don't want to be complimented on the obvious. And when you are not here, I am not always kind, considerate, and patient. I am only human, trying to do my best even if it isn't perfect. I am not a saint—and I don't want to be one.

Acknowledge that I am working hard and that I am doing my best—and that is good enough. Each one of us has a point where we have no more to give, and you need to honor that point no matter where it is. Sometimes it is enough, and sometimes it is not. We are just trying to do our best, that's all we can do.

ACKNOWLEDGMENTS

I want to thank many people who made this book possible. First, I want to thank the caregivers who donated stories about their experiences and shared emotions that are tough and tender. They are brave and generous souls.

I want to thank those who encouraged me to write these stories— Joan Hlas, Laurie Phillips, Kathy Weber, Gwen Hauser, and my parents, Jean and Philip Gangsei. I would not have been brave enough to do this without their support.

Thank you to Jon Spayde, who did a wonderful job editing my manuscript because he understood what this book is all about.

I want to thank the people at Struthers Parkinson's Center. Their resources and caring helped me every step of the way. I knew they were the place to go when I needed to move on to the next "new normal."

And most of all, I thank my husband, Gerry Glaser. For obvious reasons, this book would not have happened without him. I appreciate his willingness to let me share our stories and his generosity of spirit that makes my life with him a true gift.

THE GIFT OF A PRAYER

It's a strange life living with a person
With a disabled thought train.
It's like a sudden storm turning into a rainbow,
Giving hope and relief,
only to see another cloud on the horizon.
One has to decide how to react
To each situation as it presents itself.
So, I rejoice in the good times and cope with the unusual
With the help of God and the intellect He gives.
I feel grateful for help from children and friends
but most of all, the kind attitude of my afflicted loved one,
who even in confusion, is the kindest person I've ever known.

This prayer was donated by Helen Kuester, whose husband died of
Parkinson's. More of her poetry can be found on Barnes & Noble,
Amazon, and Publish America. Her books are *Rays of Hope* and *Through
the Window of My Heart*.

ABOUT THE COVER ART

I designed and weaved the "Burning Bush" tapestry during the time I was consumed by my role as a caregiver for my husband who had Parkinson's. For me, the Burning Bush symbolizes two things.

First, I have always identified with Moses when he stood in front of the burning bush and God told Moses he was to lead the Israelites out of Egypt. Moses did not want to do it. I didn't want to deal with my husband's Parkinson's either. Moses tried to get out of his commission several times. Who am I to do this? I am not suited for the task. Send someone else. For years I had the same conversation with God as my husband's Parkinson's progressed. Moses was not let off the hook, and neither was I.

The other meaning of the Burning Bush tapestry is that although the fire is hot and intense, it does not consume the bush. The bush remains alive to grow and produce new life. I have survived Parkinson's and, in the process, found unexpected gifts, strength I did not know I had, and a new, more meaningful life.

My tapestries have been exhibited at Luther Seminary, Basilica of Saint Mary, Nina Bliese Gallery, Vesterheim Norwegian American Museum, and Jones-Harrison assisted living and nursing facility. The Burning Bush is woven with wool warp and seine cotton weft. It is fifty inches by fifty inches in size.

ABOUT THE AUTHOR

Susan Gangsei is an author, speaker, artist, and marketing professional. She is also a family caregiver for her husband who was diagnosed with Parkinson's disease in 2000.

Susan has worked in marketing for more than thirty years—for both profit and nonprofit organizations. In 2011, she took a sabbatical to reassess both her professional and personal life.

Because of her husband's Parkinson's disease, Susan decided to structure her work life to be more flexible and to work from a home office. She reaffirmed that she loved the challenge and discipline of marketing, and that she wanted to use her expertise to help purpose-driven small businesses expand and transform themselves.

When no one is looking, Susan slips into her studio to weave. This is a place of renewal and exploration for her. Weaving became her entry point into the art world. "I've found out that I'm a creative at heart, whether it's creating new opportunities for others or an image that communicates."

The Light in the Middle of the Tunnel is Susan's first book. She can be reached at Susan@TheLightintheMiddleoftheTunnel.com.